Contributing Editor
Sara Connolly

Managing Editor
Ina Massler Levin, M.A.

Illustrator
Mark Mason

Cover Artist
Denise Bauer

Art Production Manager
Kevin Barnes

Imaging
James Edward Grace
Rosa C. See

Publisher
Mary D. Smith, M.S. Ed.

Readers' Theater
Tall Tales

Ideal for Fluency Practice

Retold by

Maureen Gerard, Ph.D.

Teacher Created Resources, Inc.
6421 Industry Way
Westminster, CA 92683
www.teachercreated.com

ISBN: 978-1-4206-3066-4

©2006 Teacher Created Resources, Inc.
Reprinted, 2007
Made in U.S.A.

Table of Contents

Introduction

The Connection between Fluency and Readers' Theater

Performance reading in the form of readers' theater is a motivating, interesting, and exciting way to include oral reading in the curriculum. Repeated reading in readers' theater is a powerful tool for developing reading fluency, particularly in the elementary grades. As teachers, we have noticed that children who read aloud in reading groups often skip ahead to preview their own passage and fail to read along with the other students. Or, the students will try to read so fast, little understanding or comprehension is possible. In contrast, oral reading in readers' theater helps to build confidence in reluctant readers. Oral reading in readers' theater strengthens decoding skills. It connects spoken and written language. It boosts comprehension, and it provides accurate, informal assessment of reading development. It is a simple educational tool for reading authentic literature in repeated practice readings that are multiple and purposeful. No costumes, props, or scenery are required unless the students and teacher wish to include them in the performance. Without movement and performance paraphernalia, children have only one attribute to make their performance meaningful and convincing…their voices.

Fluency is the ability to read quickly and accurately while at the same time using expression and proper phrasing. Fluency is particularly important when considering young children just learning to read or readers just beginning to read English. Those students who expend so much effort decoding words letter by letter decrease their understanding of the material because their attention and energy is not focused on finding meaning and sense in the text. You will notice this when, after listening to a struggling reader, you find that the student does not understand what they have just read.

Children who read more fluently use their energy and attention to focus on the meaning of the print. They comprehend what they read. The fluent reader has enough attention in reserve to make connections between the text and their own background knowledge, which gives the reader a much richer understanding of the material. When oral reading of text is more fluent, and sounds like natural speech, children are better able to pull from their own prior knowledge and experiences for comprehension.

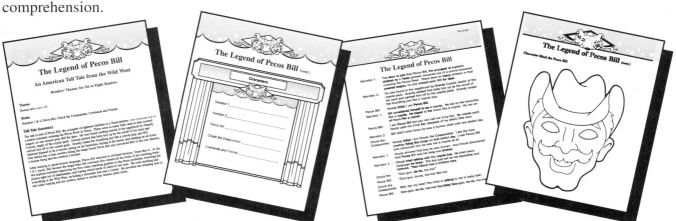

Introduction *(cont.)*

The Connection between Fluency and Readers' Theater *(cont.)*

Reading fluency does not develop quickly. As adults we have all experienced the need to reread something that we did not understand at first reading. It could have been a technical manual, a cooking recipe, or a newspaper article, but through rereading, we were able to pull the meaning from the words. Many children balk at reading a selection over again. The struggling readers, who need it most, may be particularly unmotivated. If told to read silently, these students often pretend to read, and the more advanced readers are bored by the whole notion of going through the text a second time when they feel that they understood it the first time.

The readers' theater scripts in this book include parts for several children to read together. The students are also participating in a limited form of paired reading, which is another proven fluency strategy. In paired reading, a stronger reader reads aloud with a weaker reader. By listening to the fluent reader, the weaker reader learns how the readers' voice, expression, and phrasing help to make sense of the print.

Readers' theater is not only effective in developing reading fluency, it is capable of transforming a class into excited readers. It is one activity within the school day where the struggling readers do not stand out. With teacher support and repeated practice, all students can read their lines with accuracy and expression and gain confidence in their own reading abilities. It is a simple tool that covers multiple objectives in reading instruction.

Tall Tales in American Folklore

Tall tales are a part of a larger body of traditional literature that includes stories, songs, and poems that have been passed on through oral storytelling. The authors of theses tales are unknown because of decades of telling and retelling. The timeless appeal of tall tales has made them memorable from generation to generation. Tall tales, like other traditional literature, have very clear structure, plot, rhythm, and rhyme. These stories invite active audience participation, which makes them ideal story matter for readers' theater scripts. And, many cultures still maintain a vital, strong tradition of oral story telling.

Folklore and legends abound from every time period in United States history. America was a challenging, wild new country and frontiers people of all sorts moved westward to tame the land. Wherever people settled the new frontier and worked hard to survive, tales of "larger than life" characters were told and retold. Fact and fantasy blended into a rich tradition of oral storytelling that served to entertain, to calm fears, and to offer wisdom and warnings for the challenges of frontier existence. And these tales offered outrageous explanations for the sights and sounds of the rugged, frontier terrain. Often, specific regions of the country or occupational groups created outsized champions of their way of life.

Introduction *(cont.)*

Tall Tales in American Folklore *(cont.)*

The exploits of frontiersmen in the eastern woodlands who befriended the natives and opened the new land to the earliest American settlers live on today in the stories of Davey Crockett and Daniel Boone. The lumberjacks of the wooded northlands spent long, frigid weeks harvesting trees and cutting lumber. Wielding an ax and pulling a handsaw made dangerous, backbreaking work for these adventurers. As with the settlers of the American frontier, when dark fell on the cold lumber camp and black night swallowed the woods, the lumberjacks huddled in rickety lean-to shacks around blazing stoves telling "fibs and whoppers." Today these stories are the tall tales we know of Paul Bunyan, his two-headed ax, and the blue ox, Babe.

Cowboys taming the Wild West lived the whole year riding the open ranges. Herding cattle exposed these men and women to all sorts of extreme weather and dangerous predators. Lying under the stars at night, the cowpokes sang trail songs and spun giant "yarns" to delight and entertain each other. These songs and oral stories preserve the dangers of winning the west. This folklore comes to us as the tall tales of Pecos Bill, Slue-Foot Sue, Annie Oakley, and Calamity Jane. During the nineteenth century, ribbons of railroad tied the eastern cities of the American seaboard to the open ranges and goldfields of the west. Steel driving and laying miles of track consumed thousands of man-hours and cost hundreds of lives. African American laborers exaggerated the prowess and heroic power of John Henry, the steel driving man.

Tall tales have become a unique genre of children's literature. Exaggerated accounts of American heroes with engaging illustrations find their way into classrooms and libraries across the country. The readings and scripts in this book represent some of the best-known retellings of these traditional oral stories as shared reading activities. Readers' theater gives students of all ability levels the motivation to practice fluent reading aloud. The text of the tall tale tells the story for all students to read while the readers' theater script allows several students to take turns reading parts of the text aloud.

Introduction *(cont.)*

References

Blau, Lisa, "The Power of Reader's Theater." *Scholastic Instructor*, (Jan./Feb. 2003).

Dowhower, S. L., "Effects of Repeated Reading on Second-Grade Transitional Readers Fluency and Comprehension." *Reading Research Quarterly 22*, no. 4: 389–406

Griffith, Lorraine Wieber and Timothy V. Rasinski, "A Focus on Fluency: How One Teacher Incorporated Fluency with her Reading Curriculum." *The Reading Teacher 58*, no. 2. (October 2004).

Hirsch, Jr., E.D. "Reading Comprehension Requires Knowledge of Words and the World." *American Educator* (Spring 2003).

Kuhn, M. R., and Stahl, S. A. *Fluency: A Review of Developmental and Remedial Practices*, Ann Arbor, MI: Center for the Improvement of Early Reading Achievement, (2000).

LaBerge, D., and Samuels, S.J. "Toward a Theory of Automatic Information Processing in Reading." *Cognitive Psychology*, no. 6: 293-323, (1974).

Learning Point Associates. *Reading First: A Closer Look at the Five Essential Components of Effective Reading Instruction,* 2004.

Martinez, M., Roser, N., and Strecker, S., "I Never Thought I Could Be a Star: A Readers Theater Ticket to Reading Fluency." *The Reading Teacher no.* 52: 326-334, (1999).

Introduction *(cont.)*

References *(cont.)*

Morgan, R. and Lyon, E., "Paired Reading—A Preliminary Report on a Technique for Parental Tuition of Reading-Retarded Children." *Journal of Child Psychology and Psychiatry,* 20: 151-160. (1979)

National Institute of Child Health and Human Development, Report of the National Reading Panel. *Teaching Children to Read: An Evidence-Based Assessment of the Scientific Research Literature on Reading and its Implications for Reading Instruction*, NIH Publication No. 004769, Washington, D.C.: U. S. Government Printing Office, (2000).

Rasinski, Timothy V. *The Effects of Cued Phrase Boundaries in Texts.* Bloomington, IN: ERIC Clearinghouse on Reading and Communication Skills (ED 313689), (1990).

Rasinski, Timothy V. *The Fluent Reader.* New York: Scholastic Professional Books, 2003.

Samuels, S.J., "The Method of Repeated Reading." *The Reading Teacher*, 32: 403-408, (1979).

Topping, K. , "Paired Reading: A Powerful Technique for Parent Use." *The Reading Teacher*, 40: 604-614, (1987).

Topping, K. , "Peer Tutored Paired Reading: Outcome Data from Ten Projects." *Educational Psychology*, 7: 133-145, (1987).

U.S. Department of Education, Put Reading First: *The Research Building Blocks for Teaching Children to Read,* 2001.

Standards in the Language Arts

In 1996, the National Council of Teachers of English together with the International Reading Association published a framework of standards for the English Language Arts. This framework identifies 12 broad standards that include skills and abilities for reading and writing. In 1999, Mid-Continent Research for Education and Learning published skill specific benchmarks to add detail and specificity to the official, national language arts standards developed by NCTE and IRA. The NCTE/IRA standards (**www.ncte.org/about/over/standards**) together with the McREL benchmarks (**www.mcrel.org/compendium/standards**) have been used to develop the lessons in this book. Each state has developed its own specific academic standards for students. You are urged to learn what the specific standards for the language arts domain are where you teach. The chart below shows the McREL standards for language arts for grades 3–5. The checks indicate the standards that are addressed in readers' theater.

Standard 5: Uses the general skills and strategies of the reading process	
1. Previews text (e.g., skims material; uses pictures, textual clues, and text format)	√
2. Establishes a purpose for reading (e.g., for information, for pleasure, to understand a specific viewpoint)	√
3. Represents concrete information (e.g., persons, places, things, events) as explicit mental pictures	√
4. Makes, confirms, and revises simple predictions about what will be found in a text (e.g., uses prior knowledge and ideas presented in text, illustrations, titles, topic sentences, key words, and foreshadowing clues)	√
5. Uses phonetic and structural analysis techniques, syntactic structure, and semantic context to decode unknown words (e.g., vowel patterns, complex word families, syllabication, root words, affixes)	√
6. Uses a variety of context clues to decode unknown words (e.g., draws on earlier reading, reads ahead)	√

Standards in the Language Arts *(cont.)*

Standard 5 *(cont.)*: Uses the general skills and strategies of the reading process	
7. Uses word reference materials (e.g., glossary, dictionary, thesaurus) to determine the meaning, pronunciation, and derivations of unknown words	√
8. Understands level-appropriate reading vocabulary (e.g., synonyms, antonyms, homophones, multi-meaning words)	√
9. Monitors own reading strategies and makes modifications as needed (e.g., recognizes when he or she is confused by a section of text; questions whether the text makes sense)	√
10. Adjusts speed of reading to suit purpose and difficulty of the material	√
11. Understands the author's purpose (e.g., to persuade, to inform)	
12. Uses personal criteria to select reading material (e.g., personal interest, knowledge of authors and genres, text difficulty, recommendations of others)	

Standards in the Language Arts *(cont.)*

Standard 6: Uses reading skills and strategies to understand and interpret a variety of literary text	
1. Uses reading skills and strategies to understand a variety of literary passages and texts (e.g., fairy tales, folktales, fiction, nonfiction, myths, poems, fables, fantasies, historical fiction, biographies, autobiographies, chapter books)	√
2. Knows the defining characteristics of a variety of literary forms and genres (e.g., fairy tales, folktales, fiction, nonfiction, myths, poems, fables, fantasies, historical fiction, biographies, autobiographies, chapter books)	√
3. Understands the basic concept of plot (e.g., main problem, conflict, resolution, cause-and-effect)	
4. Understands similarities and differences within and among literary works from various genres and cultures (e.g., in terms of settings, character types, events, point of view, role of natural phenomena)	√
5. Understands elements of character development in literary works (e.g., differences between main and minor characters; stereotypical characters as opposed to fully developed characters; changes that characters undergo; the importance of a character's actions, motives, and appearance to plot and theme)	√
6. Makes inferences or draws conclusions about characters' qualities and actions (e.g., based on knowledge of plot, setting, characters' motives, characters' appearances, other characters' responses to a character)	√
7. Knows themes that recur across literary works	√
8. Understands the ways in which language is used in literary texts (e.g., personification, alliteration, onomatopoeia, simile, metaphor, imagery, hyperbole, beat, rhythm)	√
9. Makes connections between characters or simple events in a literary work and people or events in his or her own life	√

Standards in the Language Arts *(cont.)*

Standard 7: Uses reading skills and strategies to understand and interpret a variety of informational texts	
1. Uses reading skills and strategies to understand a variety of informational texts (e.g., textbooks, biographical sketches, letters, diaries, directions, procedures, magazines)	√
2. Knows the defining characteristics of a variety of informational texts (e.g., textbooks, biographical sketches, letters, diaries, directions, procedures, magazines)	
3. Uses text organizers (e.g., headings, topic and summary sentences, graphic features, typeface, chapter titles) to determine the main ideas and to locate information in a text	
4. Uses the various parts of a book (e.g., index, table of contents, glossary, appendix, preface) to locate information	
5. Summarizes and paraphrases information in texts (e.g., includes the main idea and significant supporting details of a reading selection)	√
6. Uses prior knowledge and experience to understand and respond to new information	√
7. Understands the author's viewpoint in an informational text	√
8. Understands structural patterns or organization in informational texts (e.g., chronological, logical, or sequential order; compare-and-contrast; cause-and-effect; proposition and support)	√

Readers' Theater Performances

McRel Standards Benchmark: 5.1 5.10

- Reads aloud familiar stories, poems, and passages with fluency and expression (e.g., rhythm, flow, meter, tempo, pitch, tone, intonation)

Preparing

- Photocopy the tall tales scripts, one copy for each student to use for school practice and one copy for each student for home practice.
- Highlight each individual part; this may be done by the teacher in advance or by the students on their own script copy.
- Photocopy character masks to be used in performance, one mask per student.

Materials

- copies of the readers' theater scripts for each student
- Tall Tales character masks copied on cardstock, one mask per character
- crayons or markers for each student to color the cardstock character mask
- scissors for each student to cut out the cardstock mask (including the eyes) of the character he or she will enact
- a craft stick for each mask
- glue to paste masks to craft sticks
- overhead transparency of the tall tale script for whole class instruction
- highlighters to mark each individual student script
- pencils to mark each individual student script

Introducing Tall Tales

- Create background knowledge about tall tales by reading the tall tale summary aloud.
- Pre-read the tall tale script you have selected first with your students in one of these ways:

    1. You read the script aloud to the whole class using an overhead copy of the tall tale script.
    2. You read the script aloud to the whole class in Shared Reading with each student reading from a personal copy of the tall tale script.

Readers' Theater Performances *(cont.)*

Introducing Tall Tales *(cont.)*

3. Have students participate in guided reading in small groups selected by you. (Guided reading groups are small groups of children who meet with the teacher to read as the teacher guides the reading activity.)

4. Have students participate in buddy reading with two students partnered to read the tall tale script, alternating parts.

5. Have students participate in paired reading with two students partnered to read the tall tale script together at the same time.

Practice Reading

- Students can audition for the individual parts, select the parts they would like to read, or you can assign parts based on differentiated reading level of each role.

- Practice reading the tall tale script you have selected with your students in one of these ways:

   1. whole class practice while reading from individual copies of a tall tales script

   2. small group, guided reading in "performance groups" selected by you, using either the same tall tale script for each group or a different tall tale script for each group

   3. small group, independent practice reading in "performance groups"

- Use the vocabulary in the scripts to develop word study activities.

- Continued Practice Reading of the tall tale script may be done as:

   1. whole class reading from individual copies of a tall tales script

   2. small group, guided reading in "performance groups" selected by you using either the same tall tale script for each group or a different script for each group

   3. small group, independent practice reading

Reading in Character

- Final practice of the tall tale script with all students "in character"

Readers' Theater Performances *(cont.)*

Preparing for Performance

Even before you give your readers their scripts, you can help them prepare by reading them the script or its source story. Effective modeling will give them a head start against any difficulties. You might also want to discuss the difference between characters and narrators. (In the story, character parts are inside the quotation marks, and narrator parts are outside.")

Here are instructions your readers can follow—individually or in a group—to prepare their scripts and become familiar with their parts.

- Highlight your speeches in your copy of the script. Mark only words you will speak, not the identifying role tags or the stage directions. (Yellow non-fluorescent marker works best.)

- Underline the words that tell about anything you'll need to act out, words in either the stage directions or other reader's speeches. If you're given extra stage directions later, write them in the margin in pencil.

- Read through your part silently. If there are words you don't understand or aren't sure how to pronounce, look them up in a dictionary. If there are words you must remember to stress, underline them. If there are places you'll need to pause between sentences, mark them with a couple of slashes (//). For instance, a narrator must sometimes pause to help the audience know there is a change of scene or time.

- Read through your part out loud. If you're a character, think about how that character would sound. Should you try a funny voice? How would the character feel about what's happening in the story? Can you speak as if you were feeling that?

- Stand up and read through the script again. If you're a character, try out faces and movements. Would your character stand or move in a special way? Can you do that? If possible, try all this in front of a mirror.

Readers' Theater Director Hints

Rehearsing

Help your students to develop vocal power by checking their breathing. To do this, students must place their hands on their stomachs and inhale. If students are actually filling their lungs, their hands will be pushed out as they inhale. The diaphragm muscle gives the lungs more room to expand by pushing down on the stomach. If their hands move in and the stomach gets tighter, it means the students are filling only the top parts of their lungs. To help your students stand up straight, ask them to imagine a wire attached to their chest, pulling straight up to the ceiling.

- Hold your script steady, making sure it doesn't cover your mouth. If you can't see people in the front row of the audience, the script is too high.

- Try to look up often. You should keep your head still and only move you eyes.

- S-p-e-a-k s-l-o-w-l-y and c-l-e-a-r-l-y and l-o-u-d-l-y.

- Speak with feeling.

- Narrators control the story! Give all the characters enough time to say each line and to make each gesture. Generally, the narrators speak to the audience.

- Characters bring the story to life! Be in character even when not speaking. Listen to and react to the other characters' lines.

Readers' Theater Director Hints *(cont.)*

Performing

Performance day is here! Direct your students to:

- Stop speaking while the audience laughs.

- Ignore anyone who might walk in after the performance starts.

- Don't look up at anyone in the audience.

- Pretend that any mistakes were intended.

- Try to leave anything you drop on the ground until the audience is looking somewhere else.

Readers' Theater Lesson Plans

Lesson 1: Fact and Fantasy/Hyperbole

McRel Language Arts Standards Benchmark: 6.1 6.2 6.4 6.5

- Knows the difference between fact and fiction, real and make-believe

Lesson Objectives

- Students will know the defining characteristics of tall tales.
- Students will use reading skills and strategies to understand a variety of tall tales.
- Students will understand the origins of tall tales in the history of American settlement and westward expansion.
- Students will understand the use of hyperbole in tall tales.

Materials

- copies of the readers' theater scripts
- index cards

Introducing the Tall Tales Genre

Introduce the Tall Tale genre by reading aloud the summary of the legend of Paul Bunyan. Ask the students if they have ever heard of tall tales or have heard of Paul Bunyan before hearing this story. Allow students to share what they know and have heard about tall tales. Since there are many versions of tall tales, students may offer very different stories than the version here.

Understanding the Tall Tales Genre

So that your students will have an easier time understanding the tall tales genre, explain that folklore, myths, and legends are found during every time period in history. In U.S. history, wherever people settled the new frontier and worked hard to survive, oral stories of "larger than life" characters were told and retold. With each retelling, fact and fantasy blended into a rich tradition of oral storytelling that served to entertain, to calm fears, and to offer wisdom and warnings for the challenges of frontier life. And these tales offered outrageous explanations (hyperbole) for the sights and sounds of the rugged, frontier terrain. Often, specific regions of the country or occupational groups created outsized champions of their way of life.

Ask the students to decide which parts of the story are possible (fact) and which parts of the story are extremely exaggerated (fantasy). Explain to the students that in literary language, an extreme exaggeration is called a *hyperbole*. The larger than life characters and hyperbole of these stories make them into tall tales. As time allows, read summaries of the other tall tales. Discuss the literary elements of character, setting of the tale, and the natural wonders that each tall tale attempts to explain.

Readers' Theater Lesson Plans *(cont.)*

Lesson 1: Fact and Fantasy/Hyperbole *(cont)*

Assigning Roles and Creating Performance Groups

Assign roles to students based on reading level and reading proficiency. It is important to keep in mind that as students practice, fluency develops as they read materials at or below their reading level. This helps students to focus on reading accuracy, vocal expression, and reading rate. If a student is reading text that is too difficult, attention is on word recognition and decoding rather than on comprehension and fluency. Meet with each performance group as a guided reading group to monitor reading levels (see p. 13 for more on Guided Reading).   Performance groups can meet again later to practice reading and rereading the scripts for performance.

ELL Support

Encourage the English language learners in your classroom to share tall tales and extremely exaggerated stories from their own families and cultural histories. For students with very limited English skills, encourage the students to draw pictures or cartoon frames that depict the tall tales from their own cultures.

Readers' Theater Lesson Plans *(cont.)*

Lesson 2: Developing Vocabulary

McRel Language Arts Standards Benchmark: 5.6 5.7

Lesson Objectives

- Students will identify unknown vocabulary words from the readers' theater script.

- Students will use a variety of context clues to learn unknown vocabulary words from the readers' theater script.

Procedure

1. Provide each student with a copy of a tall tale script to follow along with as you read the script as a whole class. You read the script aloud to the students as they follow along. As you read the script aloud, use varying voice and expression for the different characters.

2. Have the students name words in the script which are new, unknown words for them.

3. Record all new vocabulary words found by the students onto index cards in large letters. Staple or tape the cards to the classroom word wall. (The classroom word wall is a learning tool for organizing new words that the students learn to read and write. Teachers can create a word wall on a chalkboard, bulletin board, or wall space by stapling or taping the letters of the alphabet in order to serve as headings to group the new words together.) Alternately, you record the new vocabulary words onto chart paper or on the chalkboard.

4. Use the newly created list for vocabulary word study.

ELL Support

Students who are low-level readers or ELL students would benefit greatly from hearing the script read fluently as they read along with their scripts. Have these students listen to an audio recording of the tall tale at a listening center. Provide time outside of your readers' theater lesson to allow them extra practice in paired reading with the recording.

Readers' Theater Lesson Plans *(cont.)*

Lesson 3: Instructing the Fluency Lesson Objectives/Chunking Phrases

McRel Language Arts Standards Benchmark: 5.10

- Reads aloud familiar stories, poems, and passages with fluency and expression (e.g., rhythm, flow, meter, tempo, pitch, tone, intonation)

Lesson Objectives

- Students will read the script lines fluently and accurately with an oral reading activity.

- Students will read using rhythm, flow, meter, tempo, pitch, tone, and intonation.

Procedure

When parts have been assigned and performance groups formed for the readers' theater, meet with each group as a guided reading group. (See page 13 for more about Guided Reading.) Explain to the students in the guided reading group that a major goal for readers' theater is for the students to become "unglued" from the words on the page and to be able to read the words quickly and accurately by sight.

1. Demonstrate reading that does not use correct phrasing by reading the first line from the Paul Bunyan script in a choppy, word-by-word manner. Pause at each slash (/) or phrase-cue between words.

   A long / time ago in a time too / far away for even history / books to / mention, America / was one continuous timberland.

2. Draw students' attention to the fact that the lines are very difficult to understand when you read them in this manner. Next, read the line again. Pause only at the end of each phrase-cue or at a comma as follows:

   A long time ago / in a time too far away for even history books to mention, / America was one continuous timberland.

3. Ask students to explain the difference they heard in the two readings of the first line of the script. They will probably say that the second reading of the line was easier to understand, smoother, and made more sense. Explain that the second reading used chunking of words into phrases.

Readers' Theater Lesson Plans *(cont.)*

Lesson 3: Instructing the Fluency Lesson Objectives/ Chunking Phrases *(cont)*

Procedure *(cont.)*

4. Instruct students that phrases are chunked at prepositions, conjunctions, and at the subject and predicate of a sentence. Help students to identify prepositions, conjunctions, and the subject and predicate as they read the lines of their script. Students should mark their personal scripts with a highlighter to note phrases or they can lightly mark their scripts with a pencil at pauses with a slash mark (/) to chunk phrases together.

ELL Support

While each script in this series has as few as four and up to as many as ten roles, there are other ways to involve all of your students, including those learning English. If you are not using multiple tall tales simultaneously, allow different groups of students to practice and perform the same script. This will allow all of the students an opportunity to perform a readers' theater and to practice fluent oral reading. If a group is short members, assign multiple roles to the more proficient readers.

Readers' Theater Lesson Plans *(cont.)*

Lesson 3: Instructing the Fluency Lesson Objectives *(cont.)*

Prepositions

about	between	into	through
above	beyond	like	throughout
across	but	near	till
after	by	of	to
against	concerning	off	toward
along	despite	on	under
among	down	onto	underneath
around	during	out	until
at	except	outside	up
before	excepting	over	upon
behind	for	past	with
below	from	regarding	within
beneath	in	round	without
beside	inside	since	

Conjunctions

and	whenever	because
but	either-or	unless
or	neither-nor	with exception of
nor	not-but-also	before
that	whether-or	if
when	till	once
for	while	since
so	after	until
yet	although	
both-and	as	
though	as if	

Readers' Theater Lesson Plans *(cont.)*

Lesson 4: Instructing the Fluency Lesson Objectives/Observing Punctuation, Using Intonation

McRel Language Arts Standards Benchmark: 5.10

- Reads aloud familiar stories, poems, and passages with fluency and expression (e.g., rhythm, flow, meter, tempo, pitch, tone, intonation)

Lesson Objectives

- Students will read the script, pausing to observe punctuation and use appropriate voice pitch and intonation for the punctuation used.

Procedure

When parts have been assigned and performance groups formed for the readers' theater, meet with each group as a guided reading group (see page 12 for more about Guided Reading). Explain to the students in the guided reading group that a major goal for readers' theater is for the students to become "unglued" from the words on the page and to be able to read the words quickly and accurately by sight, as if talking to a friend.

1. Demonstrate reading with proper intonation with this line:

    That's me! The greatest lumberjack ever was!

2. Repeat the reading using a question mark and a period. Ask the students what they heard in your voice quality for each type of punctuation.

3. Have students reread their lines of the script observing end punctuation. Repeat the reading using different end punctuation.

4. Demonstrate reading with different stress placed on the words in a sentence. Ask students how the stress changes the meaning of the sentence.

    *That's **me**! The **greatest** lumberjack ever was!*

    ***That's** me! The greatest **lumberjack** ever was!*

    *That's **me**! The greatest lumberjack **ever** was!*

    *That's me! The greatest lumberjack ever **was**!*

Readers' Theater Lesson Plans *(cont.)*

Lesson 4: Instructing the Fluency Lesson Objectives/Observing Punctuation, Using Intonation *(cont.)*

5. Have students reread their lines of the script, placing the stress on different words in the sentence.

6. Complete the practice reading of the script, observing and marking for punctuation, intonation, and best stress.

ELL Support

Students who are learning English as a second language will benefit from modeling of reading to observe punctuation and intonation. Echo reading will help these students to change stress and pitch, observe pauses, and chunk phrases of the text together. Choose a part from the script and read one phrase or sentence at a time as the student follows along on his or her script. Have the student echo read the same phrase or sentence exactly as you read it. Point out the part where you raise your voice at the end of a question. Read an exclamation point with strong emotion. Point out your pause at a comma, at the end of a sentence, and at the end of a paragraph. Have students explain where they have difficulties following your lead. Then have the students point out the changes they must follow in your stress, pitch, pauses, and chunking for fluent reading. Finally, have pairs of students reread together chorally, or echo read with each other after you have modeled this for them.

Readers' Theater Lesson Plans *(cont.)*

Lesson 5: Reading in Character

McRel Language Arts Standards Benchmark: 5.10

- Reads aloud familiar stories, poems, and passages with fluency and expression (e.g., rhythm, flow, meter, tempo, pitch, tone, intonation)

Lesson Objectives

- Students will read the script fluently and accurately within an oral reading activity focusing on voice quality, accent, intonation, and pitch.

  When parts have been assigned and performance groups formed for the readers' theater, meet with each group as a guided reading group (see page 12 for more about Guided Reading). Explain to the students in the guided reading group that a major goal for readers' theater is for the students to become "unglued" from the words on the page. They should be able to read the words quickly and accurately by sight, as if talking to a friend.

  1. Point out to your students that it is important to become very familiar with the lines of the script in order to read smoothly and fluently. Explain that fluency means reading quickly and expressively without choppiness. Emphasize that each character uses different ways of speaking, different accents, and different kinds of expression as they speak.

  2. Ask how the Narrator should sound in contrast to Paul. Demonstrate aloud how the two parts should sound.

  3. Discuss the possibilities for the voice qualities, accents, and intonations each character of the tall tale might be expected to use. Model the different voice characterizations for the students. (Alternately, ask the students to model aloud for the other students what they believe the characterization may sound like.)

  4. Echo read the scripts in character with students following the modeling of your voice quality, accents, and intonations. Point out when you raise your voice at the end of a question; the strong emotion as you read an exclamation; and the pause at a comma, at the end of a sentence, and at the end of a paragraph.

ELL Support

Students who are learning English as a second language will have difficulty with understanding and making sense of metaphors, similes, and idioms that are used in the script. To help these students to understand the script, take time in guided reading groups (see page 12 for more about Guided Reading) to find and explain similes and metaphors (figures of speech which compare two unlike things to clarify, to satirize, to dramatize, or to support the literary text). Idioms and clichés are word choices that are nonstandard English and will sound very unusual or odd to the second language learner. Find these figures of speech in the scripts and explain their meanings to the students.

Meet Paul Bunyan and His Blue Ox, Babe

An American Tall Tale from the North Woods

Readers' Theater for Four or More

Themes

reading roles out of character, humor

Roles

Narrator 1 and Narrator 2, Paul Bunyan, Babe

Tall Tale Summary

A long time ago, too long ago for history books to mention, when America was all one continuous timberland, Paul Bunyan was the greatest logger ever was. It took five giant storks, working overtime, to deliver that huge bundle of joy to his parents. Three hours after his birth he was reported to weigh a full eighty pounds and it is said a lumber wagon drawn by a team of oxen was Paul's baby carriage. His baby babblings were described as "sort of a cross between a buzz saw and a bass drum." He grew so fast that after one week, he was wearing his father's clothes. He would eat forty barrels of porridge just as an appetizer. A mighty giant of a man, Paul Bunyan had a wiry black beard he brushed with the treetops as he tramped through the dark wild woods. When the icy cold made Paul's breath frost, white clouds of steam billowed behind him.

Everywhere Paul went in the shadow of those trees went his best friend and companion, Babe the Blue Ox. Babe was the greatest, bluest beast ever was. Babe measured forty-two ax handles high. Paul rescued Babe, as a calf, from drowning during the Winter of Blue Snow. Babe was so strong that he could pull anything that had two ends, except Paul (Paul could never be pulled, and he could only be pushed so far). It is said that it took a crow a full day to fly from the tip of one horn to the other. Paul once used Babe to straighten out thirty miles of crooked town road. When Babe had pulled all the twists and curves straight, there were an extra twelve miles of road left over. Paul rolled it all up and gave it back to the town to use elsewhere. When Babe bellowed, his low growls shook the forests like the thunder.

Meet Paul Bunyan and His Blue Ox, Babe *(cont.)*

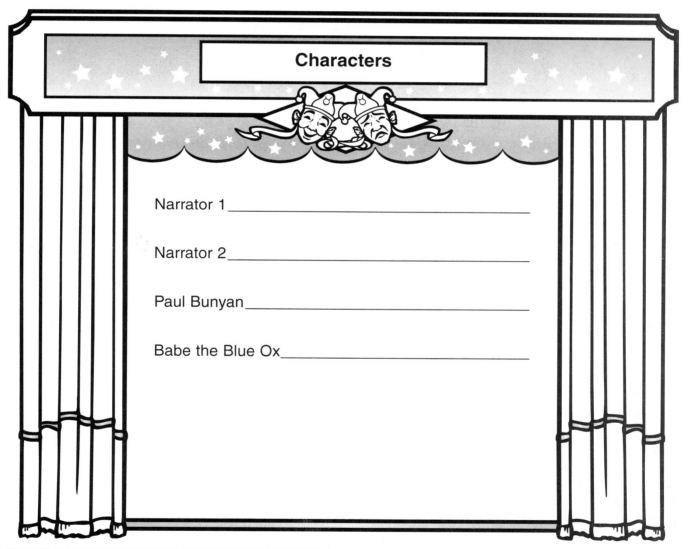

Characters

Narrator 1 _____

Narrator 2 _____

Paul Bunyan _____

Babe the Blue Ox _____

Vocabulary Word List

America	department	lumber
barrel	drowning	lumberjack
beast	forests	mighty
bellowed	giant	shining
cereal	history	storks
country	logging	wiry

Meet Paul Bunyan and His Blue Ox, Babe

Narrator 1: In a time too long ago for even history books, America was one large forest.

Narrator 2: *(Speaking to Narrator 1)* Too long ago for even history books? That was certainly a long time ago!

Narrator 1: *(sweeping gesture for "across the country")* Yes, as I was saying…thick, dark forests grew all across the country then from sea to shining sea.

Narrator 2: *(Speaking to narrator 1, not to the audience, as if truly surprised)* From sea to shining sea? That is a lot of forest!

Narrator 1: *(Clearing throat and pointing back to the audience)* AAhemm!! AAhemm!! Paul Bunyan was the greatest lumberjack there ever was.

Narrator 2: *(Speaking to Narrator 1)* From sea to shining sea? That is a lot of lumber!

Entire Cast: Paul Bunyan was a mighty, giant of a man.

Paul Bunyan: *(proudly to the audience, in loud voice)* My name is Paul Bunyan. The greatest lumberjack there ever was! I am a mighty giant of a man.

Entire Cast: Paul Bunyan was a mighty, giant of a man.

Paul Bunyan: *(proudly to the audience, in loud voice)* That's me! Paul Bunyan. I am a mighty giant of a man.

Narrator 1: Paul was so big that it took five giant storks to carry that huge bundle of joy to his parents.

Narrator 2: Five giant storks!! That is a big baby!

Meet Paul Bunyan and His Blue Ox, Babe *(cont.)*

Entire Cast: Paul Bunyan was a mighty, giant of a man.

Narrator 1: Paul Bunyan was so big that he could eat forty barrels of baby cereal.

Entire Cast: Paul Bunyan was a mighty, giant of a man.

Narrator 1: Paul was so big that he used tree tops to comb out his wiry black beard.

Narrator 2: Tree tops to comb his beard, huh? That is bigger than anything I have ever heard of.

Narrator 1: Paul was so big that on cold days his breath made steam clouds that blocked the sun all day long.

Narrator 2: I love cold mornings when I can blow puffs of steam with my breath.

Entire Cast: Paul Bunyan was a mighty, giant of a man.

Narrator 1: Everywhere Paul went in the wild north woods, Babe the Blue Ox went.

Narrator 2: Blue? I wonder why his ox was blue? What made him blue?

Paul Bunyan: *(again, proudly to the audience, in a loud voice)* Yessiree! This is my trusted friend, Babe.

Babe: That's me! I am Babe the Blue Ox. I am the greatest, bluest beast there ever was.

Entire Cast: Babe was the greatest, bluest beast ever was.

Narrator 2: *(To the entire cast)* Blue? I wonder why his ox was blue? What made him blue?

Meet Paul Bunyan and His Blue Ox, Babe *(cont.)*

Narrator 1:   *(aside as a stage direction to Narrator 2)* **Would you just read your part, please?**

Babe measured forty-two ax handles high.

Narrator 2:   **How high is an ax-handle? I don't know how high an ax-handle is.**

Narrator 1:   **It took a crow one whole day to fly between Babe's horns.**

Narrator 2:   **So, how fast do you suppose a crow flies? And does anyone know how high an ax-handle is?**

Entire Cast: **Babe is the greatest, bluest beast ever was.**

Narrator 1:   **When Babe bellowed, it shook the trees down to their roots.**

Narrator 2:   **So, how fast do you suppose a crow flies? And does anyone know how high an ax-handle is?**

Narrator 1:   *(whispering to Narrator 2)* **I think an ax-handle is about a foot and a half long.**

Narrator 2:   **So, how fast do you suppose a crow flies?**

Narrator 1:   **As I was saying . . . when Babe bellowed, it shook the trees down to their roots.**

Babe: **Some folks think they hear thunder. But, no! It was just my bellowing.**

Narrator 1:   **Paul rescued Babe as a calf. Paul saved him from freezing during the winter of Blue Snow.**

Narrator 2:   **Oh, I get it now! Babe is blue because of the blue snow. He almost froze in the blue snow. Oh, I get it now! But how fast does a crow fly?**

Entire Cast: **Babe is the greatest, bluest beast ever was.**

Narrator 2:   *(to the rest of the cast)* **You keep saying that! We understand!**

Meet Paul Bunyan and His Blue Ox, Babe *(cont.)*

Paul Bunyan: Babe is so strong that he can pull anything that has two ends.

Babe: Except Paul! And Paul will never let me push him!

Narrator 2: Babe can pull anything? I will bet Babe can't "pull our leg"!! *(slapping knee and laughing at his or her own joke)*

Entire Cast: Babe is the greatest, bluest beast ever was.

Narrator 1: Paul once used Babe to straighten out thirty miles of crooked town road.

Paul Bunyan: Babe, you are the greatest, bluest beast ever was. Now you take the end of this crooked road and pull.

Entire Cast: Babe is the greatest, bluest beast ever was. Pull, Babe, pull! Pull, Babe, pull!

Paul Bunyan: Pull, Babe, pull! Pull, Babe, pull!

Narrator 1: Babe is so strong that he can pull anything that has two ends. Babe pulled and pulled. He pulled and pulled.

Narrator 2: I wonder what our P.E. teacher would say to that? This sounds like a rope pull to me.

Narrator 1: When Babe had pulled all the twists and curves straight, there were an extra twelve miles of road left over.

Babe: Paul rolled it all up and gave it back to the town to use elsewhere.

Narrator 2: Does the city planning department know this story?

Entire Cast: Paul Bunyan is a mighty giant of a man. Babe is the greatest, bluest beast ever was.

Narrator 2: You said that before! We understand! Paul Bunyan is a mighty, giant of a man. Babe is the greatest, bluest beast ever was.

Meet Paul Bunyan and His Blue Ox, Babe *(cont.)*

Character Mask for Paul Bunyan

Meet Paul Bunyan and His Blue Ox, Babe *(cont.)*

Character Mask for Babe, the Blue Ox

The Legend of Paul Bunyan and the Talking Tools

An American Tale from the North Woods

Readers' Theater for 10 Readers

Theme

Thankfulness

Roles

Narrator 1 & 2, Paul Bunyan, Johnny Inkslinger, Big Swede, Creampuff Patty, Pen, Ax Handle, Flapjack Flipper, Babe

Suggested Props

a large pen, a stick or handle, a pancake turner

Tall Tale Summary

Johnny Inkslinger was the timekeeper at Paul Bunyan's logging camp. One amazing day, while Johnny Inkslinger was figuring the timecards, his ink pen spoke out loud to him. Johnny ran in bewilderment to Big Swede, the foreman, to tell him about the talking pen. Big Swede guffawed at the wild story until his massive ax handle yelled out, "It could happen to you!"

Startled and amazed at this turn of events, Johnny Inkslinger and Big Swede ran to Creampuff Patty, the camp cook, with the incredible tale of talking pens and ax handles. As she tried to shoo the men away, her spoon spoke to her.

Even more startled and amazed, Johnny Inkslinger, Big Swede, and Creampuff Patty ran to Paul Bunyan, with their incredible tale. Paul patiently listened to the wild stories, but scolded the three for disturbing the peace of the logging camp with their tall tales and sent them all back to their work. While Paul sat and considered the ridiculous tale he had just heard, his blue ox, Babe, lifted his giant head from drinking from the Round River and asked Paul, "Can you imagine anything sillier than a talking pen?"

The Legend of Paul Bunyan and the Talking Tools *(cont.)*

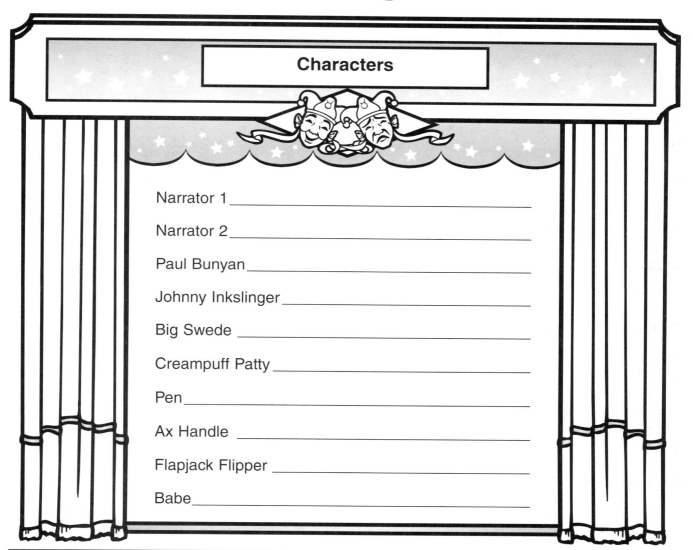

Characters

Narrator 1 _____

Narrator 2 _____

Paul Bunyan _____

Johnny Inkslinger _____

Big Swede _____

Creampuff Patty _____

Pen _____

Ax Handle _____

Flapjack Flipper _____

Babe _____

Vocabulary Word List

astonishment	delicious	logging	timecard
axhandle	fibsters	lumberjacks	thankfulness
barrel	figuring	scolding	ungrateful
book keeper	flapjacks	soggy	
bully	foreman	sling	
companion	incredible	syrup	

The Legend of Paul Bunyan and the Talking Tools

Narrator 1: Paul Bunyan was the greatest lumberjack there ever was.

Paul Bunyan: *(proudly to the audience, in loud voice)* That's me! The greatest lumberjack there ever was!

Narrator 2: Paul Bunyan has seven hundred men logging with him in the North Woods.

Narrator 1: *(to the audience)* Meet Johnny Inkslinger, the bookkeeper. He is such a fine one to figure numbers that his pens are made of peeled, sharpened trees.

Johnny Inkslinger: I am Johnny Inkslinger, and I sling ink faster than anyone can!

Narrator 1: To total up his numbers, Johnny has to dip those fine figuring pens into giant pickle barrels of ink.

Narrator 2: *(to the audience)* This is Big Swede, the bully foreman.

Big Swede: *(with a slow, deep voice)* I am Big Swede. I am the bully foreman. I am big, and my legs are as big and round as a tree trunk.

Narrator 1: His legs looked so much like tree trunks that the regular lumberjacks become confused and go after him with their saws and axes.

Narrator 2: *(to the audience)* This is the camp cook, Creampuff Patty.

Creampuff Patty: I am Creampuff Patty. Flipping flapjacks is my speciality.

Narrator 1: She flips flapjacks so light and delicious, the hungry lumberjacks have to nail down their breakfast to pour on the maple syrup.

Creampuff Patty: Have you ever seen a stack of seven hundred flapjacks? It needs a mountain of butter and barrels of maple syrup.

The Legend of Paul Bunyan and the Talking Tools *(cont.)*

Narrator 2: One amazing day, Johnny Inkslinger was figuring the timecards for all seven hundred bully men in the logging camp.

Johnny Inkslinger: There are seven hundred lumberjacks in this logging camp.

I figure each lumberjack's work hours exactly to the minute.

I don't miss dotting an i or crossing a t.

Pen: *(hidden from view of the audience)* What do you mean? I dot the i's and cross the t's!

Johnny Inkslinger: *(looking at his pen in astonishment)* Huh! Did you just say something to me? Naw! I must be hearing things.

I must need a break from figuring.

Pen: *(in exasperated tone of voice)* I said, "I dot the i's and cross the t's." If it weren't for me, you couldn't do all this figuring.

Johnny Inkslinger: *(looking at his pen in astonishment)* My peeled, sharpened tree pen is talking to me! I never heard of such a thing in all my days!

Pen: You are so ungrateful! You are never thankful for me.

Johnny Inkslinger: Oh my! My pen is scolding me. Big Swede has got to hear this. This is the most unheard of thing I ever heard of!

Narrator 1: Johnny Inkslinger ran to Big Swede, the bully foreman. He told him about the talking pen.

Narrator 2: Johnny Inkslinger didn't like the tone of voice that pen used with him either!

The Legend of Paul Bunyan and the Talking Tools *(cont.)*

Big Swede: Why are you in such a rush, Johnny Inkslinger? The last time I saw you looking so worried, your ink barrels had gone dry during tax season!

Johnny Inkslinger: Big Swede, Big Swede! You won't believe your ears. You never heard of such a thing in all your days! My peeled, sharpened tree pen is talking to me!

Big Swede: *(laughing hard and loud)* Can this be true? You have been figuring timecards too long today.

Johnny Inkslinger: And I don't like the tone of voice that pen took with me either. My pen scolded me. I sling ink faster than anyone can!

Big Swede: *(still laughing)* I don't hear a sound from your pen, Johnny Inkslinger! You have been figuring too long today.

Johnny Inkslinger: It is true! It is true, Big Swede! My peeled, sharpened tree pen talked to me.

Ax handle: *(also out of sight of the audience with the pen, very slowly)* It could happen to you!

Big Swede: *(looking at his ax handle in astonishment)* Huh! Can this be true? Did I hear my ax handle just speak?

Narrator 1: Johnny Inkslinger and Big Swede were startled and amazed at the talking pen and the talking ax handle. They ran to find Creampuff Patty to tell her the incredible tale.

Narrator 2: Creampuff Patty listened to the wild yarns. She thought the two loggers had been out in the hot sun too long.

Creampuff Patty: Can this be true? You two boys sure do need a break. You have been out in the hot sun too long today.

The Legend of Paul Bunyan and the Talking Tools *(cont.)*

Johnny Inkslinger and Big Swede: It is true! It is true, Creampuff Patty!

Johnny Inkslinger: My peeled, sharpened tree pen talked to me.

Big Swede: And my ax handle spoke to me!

Creampuff Patty: *(shooing the two away)* I don't hear a sound from your pen, Johnny Inkslinger! And I don't hear a sound from your ax handle, Big Swede. You have been out in the hot sun too long today.

Flapjack Flipper: *(also out of sight of the audience with the pen, ax handle)* I would sure run off if I were those two fools! But after all the stirring and flipping I do for you, you might just be a little more thankful for me, too.

Creampuff Patty: *(looking at her flipper in astonishment)* Huh! Can this be true? Did I hear my flapjack flipper speak?

Johnny Inkslinger: and Big Swede: It is true! It is true, Creampuff Patty!

Johnny Inkslinger: My peeled, sharpened tree pen talked to me.

Big Swede: And my ax handle spoke to me!

Creampuff Patty: And my flapjack flipper spoke to me!

Johnny Inkslinger and Big Swede and Creampuff Patty: We have got to go tell Paul Bunyan!

Narrator 1: Johnny Inkslinger, Big Swede, and Creampuff Patty ran to tell Paul Bunyan the incredible tale. Talking pens! Talking ax handles! Talking flapjack flippers!

The Legend of Paul Bunyan and the Talking Tools *(cont.)*

Narrator 2:	Paul listened to the wild stories.
Paul Bunyan:	Can this be true? You need to get back to doing your work. You are disturbing the peace of the logging camp with your tall tales.
Johnny Inkslinger and Big Swede and Creampuff Patty:	It is true! It is true, Paul Bunyan!
Johnny Inkslinger:	My peeled, sharpened tree pen talked to me.
Big Swede:	And my ax handle spoke to me!
Creampuff Patty:	And my flapjack flipper spoke to me!
Paul Bunyan:	I don't hear a sound from your pen, Johnny Inkslinger! And I don't hear a sound from your ax handle, Big Swede. And I don't hear a sound from your flapjack flipper, Creampuff Patty. No more fibbing today.
Narrator 1:	Paul Bunyan sent the three fibsters back to work.
Narrator 2:	Now Paul Bunyan's most trusted companion, Babe the Blue Ox was nearby.
Babe:	Can you imagine anything sillier than a talking pen?
Narrator 1:	Paul was scared out of his skin to hear the ox speak. Paul ran off in a fright.
Narrator 2:	Folks say the ground was soggy from the spring thaw. Paul's footprints made deep holes as he took off running through the woods.
Narrator 1:	The spring rains came and filled those footprints up with water. The footprints made 10,000 lakes in the north woods.
Narrator 2:	Johnny Inkslinger and Big Swede and Creampuff Patty were much more thankful for the tools of their trade from that day on!

The Legend Paul Bunyan and the Talking Tools *(cont.)*

Character Mask for Big Swede

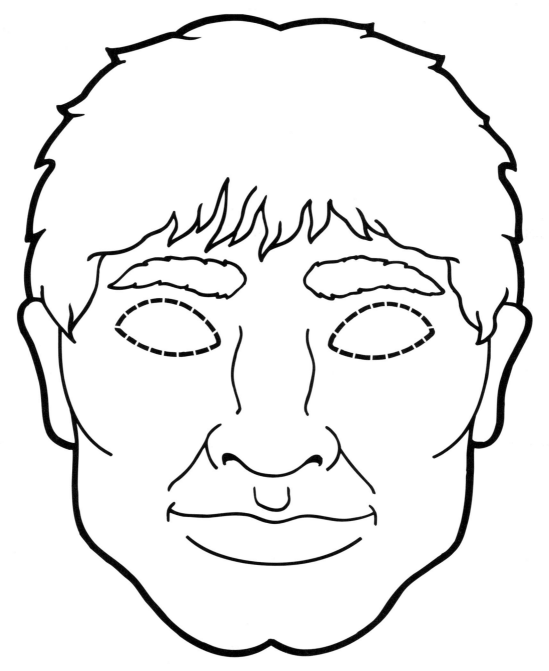

The Legend of Paul Bunyan
and the Talking Tools *(cont.)*

Character Mask for Johnny Inkslinger

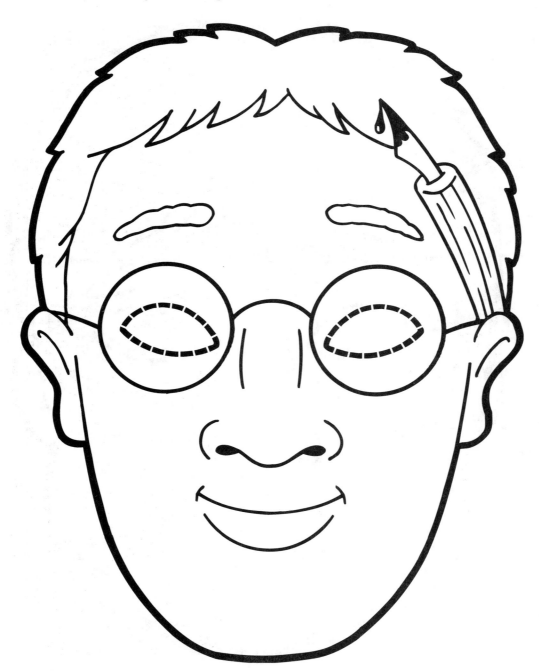

The Legend of Paul Bunyan
and the Talking Tools *(cont.)*

Character Mask for Creampuff Patty

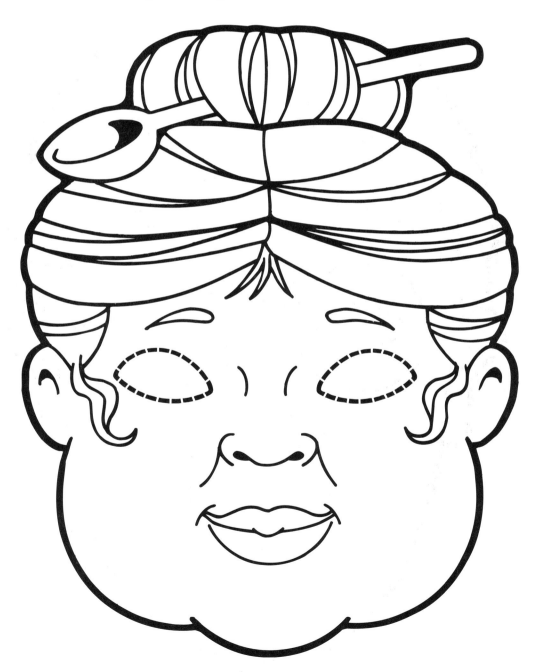

The Legend of Pecos Bill

An American Tall Tale from the Wild West

Readers' Theater for Six to Eight Readers

Theme

Honest labor pays off.

Roles

Narrator 1 & 2, Pecos Bill, Chuck the Cowpuncher, Cowhands and Friends

Tall Tale Summary

The tale is told of Pecos Bill, the youngest of eighteen children to a Texas pioneer, who bounced out of a prairie schooner crossing the Pecos River in Texas. There were so many little ones in that covered wagon, no one missed poor Bill for days. He was found rustling around in the sagebrush by Grandy Coyote, leader of the coyote pack. Grandy picked that baby boy up by the scruff of his neck and carried him off to the coyote pack. Grandy raised the foundling just like a coyote pup, and Bill believed himself to be a coyote, sitting on his haunches, baying at the moon, and running on all fours. One fateful day a lone cowboy riding the range found Pecos Bill and convinced Bill of his true identity, a human being and the cowboy's brother.

After learning to speak human language, Pecos Bill returned to civilized territory, Texas that is. At the I X L ranch, Bill became the larger-than-life cowhand who created all the tricks of the ranching trade. His exploits included organizing the first rodeo, teaching gophers to dig fence postholes, wrestling the poison right out of rattlesnakes, and roping whole herds of cattle at one time. He rode anything and everything in the Wild West, including a mountain lion and a twister. He invented the branding iron to end cattle rustling and the cowboy ballad to soothe the restless cattle herds.

The Legend of Pecos Bill *(cont.)*

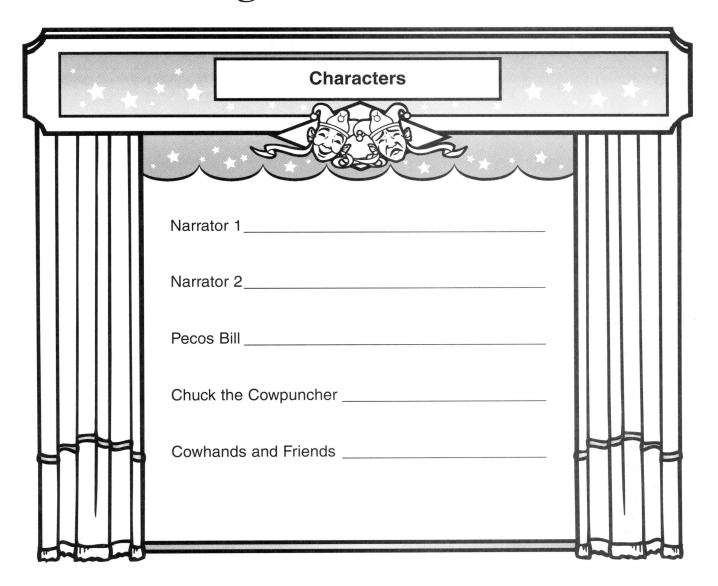

Characters

Narrator 1 _____

Narrator 2 _____

Pecos Bill _____

Chuck the Cowpuncher _____

Cowhands and Friends _____

The Legend of Pecos Bill *(cont.)*

Vocabulary Word List	
alongside	lone
brilliant	pioneer
bronco	poison
civilization	postholes
convinced	prairie
coyote	rattlesnake
covered wagon	rhyme
cowhands	rodeo
cowpoke	roundup
cowpuncher	saddle
cultured	sagebrush
fateful	schooner
foundling	scruff
gophers	steers
haunches	stallion
lasso	

The Legend of Pecos Bill

Narrator 1: The story is told that Pecos Bill, the youngest of eighteen children to a Texas pioneer, bounced out of a prairie schooner crossing the Pecos River. There were so many children in that covered wagon, no one missed poor Bill for days.

Narrator 2: He was found in the sagebrush by Grandy Coyote, leader of the coyote pack. Grandy picked that baby boy up by the scruff of his neck and carried him off to the coyote pack. Grandy raised the foundling just like a coyote pup.

Pecos Bill: Howdy folks! I am Pecos Bill.

Narrator 1: Bill considered himself to be a coyote. He sat on his haunches like a coyote. He bayed at the moon like a coyote. He ran on all fours like a coyote.

Pecos Bill: I am Pecos Bill but you can call me Crop Ear. My coyote pack family calls me Crop Ear, because of my short, little ears.

Narrator 2: Bill didn't even know he was a human child until one fateful day.

Chuck the Cowpuncher: Howdy folks! I am Chuck, the Cowpuncher. I am the lone cowboy riding the range on that fateful day. I met Pecos Bill and convinced him he was not a coyote at all.

Narrator 1: Chuck showed that boy he was human. And Chuck discovered that Pecos Bill was his long lost brother.

Narrator 2: Chuck tried talking with the coyote boy. He tried every language he knew. The boy just sat on his haunches and listened. Then Chuck had a brilliant idea.

Chuck the: "Goo-goo, da-da, ma-ma!"

Pecos Bill: "Goo-goo, da-da, ma-ma! Ma-ma!

Chuck the Cowpuncher: Well, tan my hide! The child is talking to me in baby talk!

Pecos Bill: Goo-goo, da-da, ma-ma! Itsy-bitsy! Goo-goo, da-da, ma-ma!

The Legend of Pecos Bill *(cont.)*

Narrator 1:	Chuck kept speaking to Bill in baby talk. Soon Pecos Bill started learning to put two words together. Then Pecos Bill began to make sentences. Then Pecos Bill began to sing nursery rhymes. By sundown, Pecos Bill mastered cultured English.

Chuck the Cowpuncher:	(*with the accent of highbrow British*) The rain in Spain falls mainly on the plain.

Pecos Bill:	(*with the accent of highbrow British*) The rain in Spain falls mainly on the plain.

All the cowhands and friends:	(*with the accent of highbrow British*) The rain in Spain falls mainly on the plain.

Chuck the Cowpuncher:	Yippee, ti-yee! You are the fastest at learning anything that I ever did see, Bill. You must return to Texas and civ-i-lization with me.

Pecos Bill:	But where will I live? What will I do in civ-i-lization?

Chuck the Cowpuncher:	Come to live on my ranch with me. The I X L ranch is deep in the heart of Texas. A cowboy's work is honest work.

Pecos Bill:	I will miss my life in the wild and my coyote brothers. But it is my duty to return to the human race. And I must work hard at a cowboy's work.

Narrator 1:	The cowhands at the I X L ranch were amazed by Pecos Bill. He never roped a cow. Pecos Bill just told the cow politely what he wanted in cow language. Pecos Bill never rode on a horse; Pecos Bill ran alongside the horse on all fours.

Narrator 2:	Pecos Bill found new ways to be a cowpoke at the I X L ranch. He taught the gophers to dig fence postholes for him. Pecos Bill wrestled the poison right out of rattlesnakes. Then Pecos Bill used those rattlesnakes just like a lasso to rope steers.

The Legend of Pecos Bill *(cont.)*

Narrator 1: Pecos Bill found new ways to have fun with the cowhands at I X L ranch. After every roundup of the herds from the range, Pecos Bill had a big party for all the cowboys. He called it a rodeo.

Pecos Bill: My favorite rodeo event is the bronco riding. There ain't no cowpuncher can stay on my horse, the Widow Maker. That mustang is the wildest, proudest stallion there ever was.

Chuck the Cowpuncher: There ain't no cowpuncher can stay on the Widow Maker. We call that horse the Widow Maker because every cowhand that has ever tried riding the wild white pony leaves his wife a widow.

Pecos Bill: Once, a mean old cuss of a cowhand named Old Satan tried riding Widow Maker. Widow Maker bucked Old Satan so hard he flew over the moon and landed on Pike's Peak.

The Legend of Pecos Bill (cont.)

Character Mask for Pecos Bill

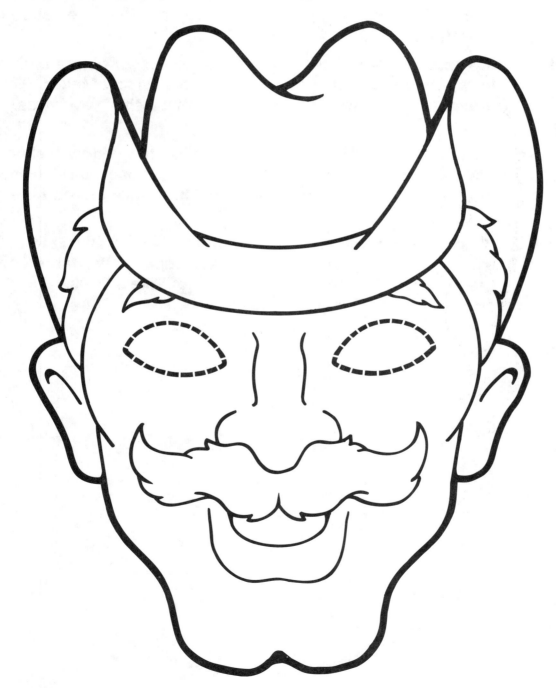

The Legend of Pecos Bill *(cont.)*

Character Mask for Chuck the Cowpuncher

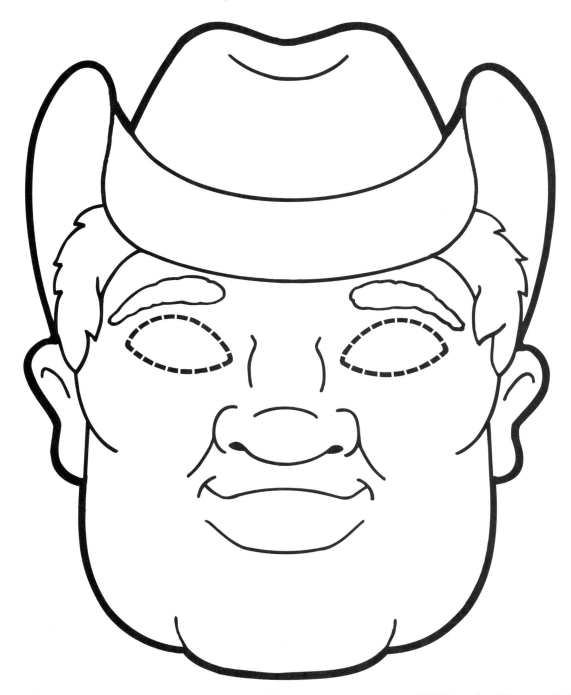

The Legend of Slue-Foot Sue, Pecos Bill's Bouncing Bride

An American Tall Tale from the Wild West

Readers' Theater for Six to Eight Readers

Theme

Stubbornness has serious consequences.

Roles

Narrator 1 & 2, Pecos Bill, Slue-Foot Sue, Cowhands and Friends

Tall Tale Summary

Now, Pecos Bill had a way with the ladies. But his one true love was Slue-Foot Sue. She could ride as well as Bill himself. Bill first saw Slue-Foot Sue riding a catfish down the Rio Grande River. She was riding standing up on that catfish and holding on with only one hand. She and her catfish made a pattern in the river water, too. Bill went head over heels for Slue-Foot Sue and proposed marriage to her on the spot. Sue dressed in a white trail train dress with a big bustle on their wedding day. She looked plumb gorgeous in that gown. Right after they got married, Sue demanded Pecos Bill prove how deep his love for her was by letting her ride his wild steed, Widow-maker. Knowing this would be disastrous, Bill tried to talk her out of it. All of the ranch hands tried to talk Sue out of it. But no! Sue climbed on that great devil of a horse.

Well, Widow-Maker bucked like a maniac. Sue was thrown off—clear up to the clouds. Luckily, Sue was still wearing her bustled trail train gown. When she hit the ground, bustle first, she bounced up again like she had hit a giant spring. Bill soon realized Sue couldn't stop bouncing. She bounced so high she kept hitting her head on the moon. She was crying and crying buckets of tears, and throwing kisses to her new husband. But even he couldn't stop her bouncing. Pecos Bill waited three days and four nights. Finally, even Bill realized that she would starve to death before she stopped bouncing.

The Legend of Slue-Foot Sue, Pecos Bill's Bouncing Bride *(cont.)*

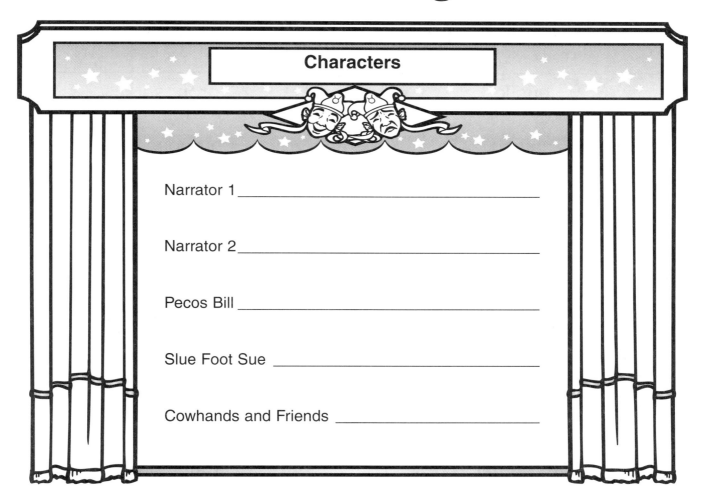

Characters

Narrator 1 _____

Narrator 2 _____

Pecos Bill _____

Slue Foot Sue _____

Cowhands and Friends _____

The Legend of Slue-Foot Sue, Pecos Bill's Bouncing Bride *(cont.)*

Vocabulary Word List	
bustle	proposal
catfish	proposed
dainty	saddle
finery	stallion
foundling	steed
glorious	stirrup
gorgeous	teacup
jim dandy	trail train
manners	waist
mustang	waltz
plumb	

The Legend of Slue-Foot Sue, Pecos Bill's Bouncing Bride *(cont.)*

Narrator 1: Now, Pecos Bill had a way with the ladies, no doubt about it. But his one true love was Slue-foot Sue. She could ride as well as Bill himself could.

Slue-foot Sue: Hi there, everyone. I am Slue-foot Sue.

Narrator 2: Bill first saw Slue-foot Sue riding a catfish down the Rio Grande River. She was riding standing up and holding on with only one hand. She and her catfish made a right pretty pattern in the river water, too.

Slue-foot Sue: Bill went head over heels for me and proposed marriage to me on the spot.

Pecos Bill: Slue-foot Sue, I can see you are a girl of talent. Would you do me the honor of becoming my wife?

Slue-foot Sue: I accept on one condition, Pecos Bill. You have been a coyote foundling and cowpuncher all your life. You must learn some proper manners.

Narrator 1: So Sue taught Pecos Bill how to balance a teacup, bow at his waist, and to waltz like a fine English gentleman.

All the Cowhands and Friends: La-dee-da, dearie me, ain't that Bill a fine jim dandy.

Narrator 2: And when their wedding day arrived, Sue dressed in the fanciest city finery that could be found.

Pecos Bill: Slue-foot Sue, you are a vision of pure beauty. You are plumb gorgeous in that gown. I promise to grant you any wish you make when you are my bride.

Slue-foot Sue: Thank you, Bill. This white satin gown is the latest fashion in the big city. It is a trail train gown. (Turning around as if to show off the back of a dress) Look here. Its chief glory is this bustle.

All the Cowhands and Friends: There ain't no cowpuncher can stay on the Widow Maker.

The Legend of Slue-Foot Sue, Pecos Bill's Bouncing Bride *(cont.)*

Narrator 1: A bustle, for those of you in the audience that have never heard of a bustle, is a wire contraption under the back of the dress that makes the skirt stand way out.

Slue-foot Sue: It is considered very handsome these days to wear a bustle. It is glorious, ain't it?

All the Cowhands and Friends: La-dee-da, dearie me, ain't that gown just something!

Pecos Bill: Could we get on with it? Is this wedding going to proceed or are we going to stand here and gab about trail train gowns with bustles all day long?

Slue-foot Sue: Proceed, of course!

Narrator 2: Slue-foot Sue remembered that Pecos Bill had promised to grant her every wish once they were married.

Narrator 1: And Sue had wished for something very devilish for a long time. She begged Pecos Bill to let her ride that wild stallion, The Widow Maker.

Slue-foot Sue: Oh please! Please, please, Bill! Let me ride The Widow Maker.

Pecos Bill: No! No! I can't let you.

Slue-foot Sue: (stamping foot angrily) Oh please! Please, please Bill! You promised to grant my every wish, Bill. And I wish to ride the Widow Maker.

Pecos Bill: No! No! I can't let you. I promised The Widow Maker to never let anyone in the saddle except me.

All the Cowhands and Friends: Don't do it! We're warning you. Don't do it!

Slue-foot Sue: I demand that you prove how deep your love for me is by letting me ride your wild steed, Widow Maker. You promised to grant my every wish.

Pecos Bill: No! No! I can't let you. I promised The Widow Maker to never let anyone in the saddle except me before I ever met you, Sue.

The Legend of Slue-Foot Sue, Pecos Bill's Bouncing Bride *(cont.)*

All the Cowhands and Friends: Don't do it! We're warning you. Don't do it!

Narrator 2: Yes folks. You guessed it. Sue dashed over to that mustang and placed her dainty white slipper in Widow Maker's stirrup.

Narrator 1: Yes folks. You guessed it. Widow Maker arched his back and bucked Sue so hard she flew right over the moon.

Pecos Bill: Catch her! Catch her, boys!

All the Cowhands and Friends: We all said, "Don't do it! We're warning you. Don't do it!"

Narrator 2: The boys spread themselves out in a wide circle. Down, down, down came Slue-foot Sue. But the boys missed.

Narrator 1: Sue hit the ground with a terrible thud. Right on her bustle.

All the Cowhands and Friends: We all said, "Don't do it! We're warning you. Don't do it!"

Narrator 2: The wire in that bustle acted just like a spring. Sue bounced right back up again into the clouds and over the moon.

Narrator 1: Up and down, up and down between the ranch and the moon bounced Slue-foot Sue. This went on for days and days.

Narrator 2: One by one the cowhands and the friends in the wedding party got tired and hungry. They wandered away while Sue kept going up and down. Up and down on that bustle.

Pecos Bill: Slue-foot Sue, I can't wait for you to stop bouncing. You are going to starve before that bustle gives out. I am sorry my dear, but I can't wait for you to stop bouncing.

Narrator 1: She was crying and crying buckets of tears, and throwing kisses to her new husband. But even he couldn't stop her bouncing.

The Legend of Slue-Foot Sue, Pecos Bill's Bouncing Bride *(cont.)*

Character Mask for Slue-Foot Sue

John Henry, Mighty Steel-Driving Man

An American Tall Tale from the Deep South

Readers' Theater for Six to Eight Readers

Theme

Man is mightier than machine.

Roles

Narrator 1 & 2, John Henry, The Blacksmith, The Foreman, The Salesman, The Crowd

Tall Tale Summary

Way down south, folks still talk about the famous railroader, John Henry. This giant of a man vowed he would drive a steel drill deeper into the rock than any machine could "even if I have to die with a hammer in my hand!" The legend of John Henry really started when he was building the railroads by driving steel on endless miles of track. John Henry was the champion of them all and would beat any challenger at driving steel.

One dark day, a salesman from the city brought a new-fangled invention that was made of steel and driven by a steam engine. He boasted that his new-fangled invention would drive through the mountain faster than any crew of men could. John Henry was certain that he could drive steel faster than any steam machine. The contest would last just one hour. The one that drilled deepest into the rock wall of the tunnel would win.

The race was on. Muscle against steam. The machine pulled ahead and bored into the rock faster and deeper than John Henry could. The machine sputtered and spit. The drill to the steam machine was jammed into the rock.

The machine operator tried to jerk the drill out of the rock. He tried cleaning out the dust. With a swifter, faster stroke, John Henry caught up with the stalled machine. John Henry swung harder and harder, up and down with everything he had, until the hour was done. He had driven into the rock farther than the machine. John Henry slumped down on the pile of rock around his feet, dead. The giant of a man lived up to his vow; he would drive a steel drill deeper into the rock than any machine could "even if I have to die with a hammer in my hand!"

John Henry, Mighty Steel-Driving Man *(cont.)*

Characters

Narrator 1 _____

Narrator 2 _____

John Henry _____

The Blacksmith _____

The Foreman _____

The Salesman _____

The Crowd _____

John Henry, Mighty Steel Driving Man *(cont.)*

Vocabulary Word List	
barges	invention
beams	locomotive
blacksmith	overseeing
champion	poled
challenge	railroaders
citizen	sheep nose
drill	shoveled
foreman	steeldrivers
Hercules	vowed

John Henry, Mighty Steel Driving Man

Narrator 1: Way down south, folks still talk about the famous railroader, John Henry.

Narrator 2: The giant of a man vowed he would drive a steel drill deeper into the rock than any machine could.

John Henry: I am John Henry, a mighty giant of a man. I vow to drive a steel drill deeper into rock than any machine "even if I have to die with a hammer in my hand."

Narrator 1: No one is quite sure where John Henry came from.

Narrator 2: Many families claimed him as a son. Several southern states claimed him as a citizen. Several cities claimed John Henry died there—and at different times.

Narrator 1: But no one is quite sure where John Henry came from.

Narrator 2: John Henry could do anything. He had picked cotton. He had poled barges up the Mississippi River. He had shoveled coal for locomotive engines.

Narrator 1: But the legend of John Henry really started when he was building the railroads by driving steel on endless miles of track.

Narrator 2: When it came to swinging a hammer and driving steel, no one could outdo John Henry. He was as big as Hercules. He was solid as a steel beam.

John Henry: I swing a 20-pound sheep-nose hammer. I sing in a deep voice and swing my mighty hammer to the rhythm of the song. I am a mighty, steel-driving man.

Blacksmith: I am the blacksmith who makes the sharpened drills for John Henry to drive with his hammer. I need six men running drills back and forth to keep John Henry supplied. He is a mighty, steel-driving man.

John Henry, Mighty Steel Driving Man *(cont.)*

Foreman: I am the foreman overseeing the railroad. John Henry can swing a hammer harder than an Alabama mule could kick. He is a mighty, steel-driving man.

The Crowd: We are the steel drivers who work alongside of John Henry. John Henry swings two 20-pound sheep-nose hammers at a time, one in each hand. He is a mighty, steel-driving man.

Narrator 1: John Henry was the champion of them all and could beat any challenger at driving steel.

Narrator 2: One dark day, a salesman from the city came around when a tunnel was being bored through the mountains. The tunnel was to be a mile and a quarter long through solid rock.

Salesman: Step right up! See the invention that can drive through this mountain faster than any man can! Step right up!

Foreman: John Henry is leading a crew hammering, driving, and blasting the tunnel through the mountain. A machine would be cheaper! Easier! Safer!

Salesman: Step right up! This steel-driving machine is made of steel and driven by a steam engine. This machine is cheaper! Easier! Safer!

John Henry: I vow to drive a steel drill deeper into rock than any machine "even if I have to die with a hammer in my hand." I challenge this steel-driving machine to a contest.

The Crowd: A challenge! A challenge! Man against machine.

Foreman: The contest will last just one hour. Man against machine.

Salesman: The one that drills deepest into the rock wall of the tunnel wins. Man against machine.

John Henry, Mighty Steel Driving Man *(cont.)*

John Henry: Man against machine. I vow to drive a steel drill deeper into rock than any machine " even if I have to die with a hammer in my hand."

Narrator 1: Man against machine. John Henry picked up his hammer with gnarled hands while the machine operator dug his feet into the dirt to support the steam machine. Ready, Set, Go!

Narrator 2: Man against machine. John Henry swung his hammer and sparks flew. Hissing and spitting the steam machine pounded against the rock too.

Narrator 1: Man against machine. The race was on. Muscle against steam.

Blacksmith: Muscle against steam. The machine has pulled ahead. It bored into the rock faster and deeper than John Henry can.

Foreman: Muscle against steam. The ground is trembling as John Henry bangs at the rock with mighty blows.

Salesman: Muscle against steam. My machine bores into the rock faster and deeper than John Henry can.

Narrator 1: Then it happened! The machine sputtered and spit.

Narrator 2: It choked and coughed. The drill to the steam machine jammed into the rock.

Foreman: Look! John Henry is pounding with a swifter, faster stroke. John Henry is catching up with the machine.

Blacksmith: Look! John Henry is swinging harder and harder, up and down with everything in him.

John Henry, Mighty Steel Driving Man *(cont.*

Salesman: The contest is not over until the hour is up.

Foreman: Look! He has driven into the rock farther than the machine.

The Crowd: Man wins against machine! Man wins against machine!

Narrator 1: The exhausted John Henry slumped down on the pile of rock around his feet.

Narrator 2: The giant of a man lived up to his vow; he would drive a steel drill deeper into the rock than any machine could "even if I have to die with a hammer in my hand."

Narrator 1: Man wins against machine! The giant of a man died with his hammer in his hand.

John Henry, Mighty Steel Driving Man *(cont.)*

Character Mask for John Henry

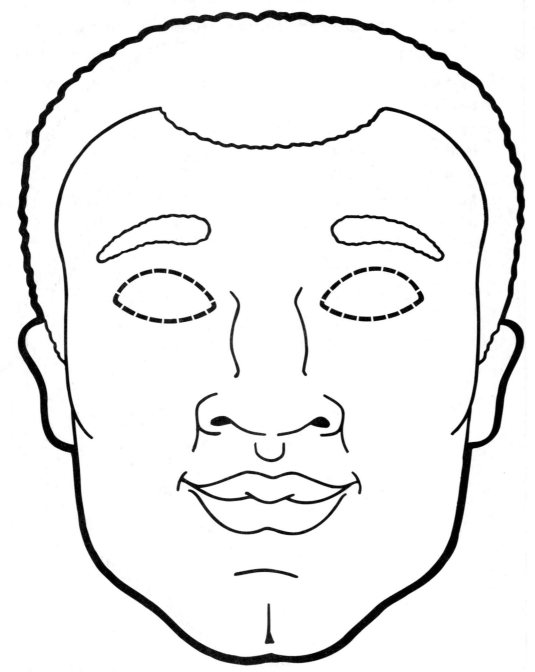

John Henry, Mighty Steel Driving Man *(cont.)*

Character Mask for Foreman

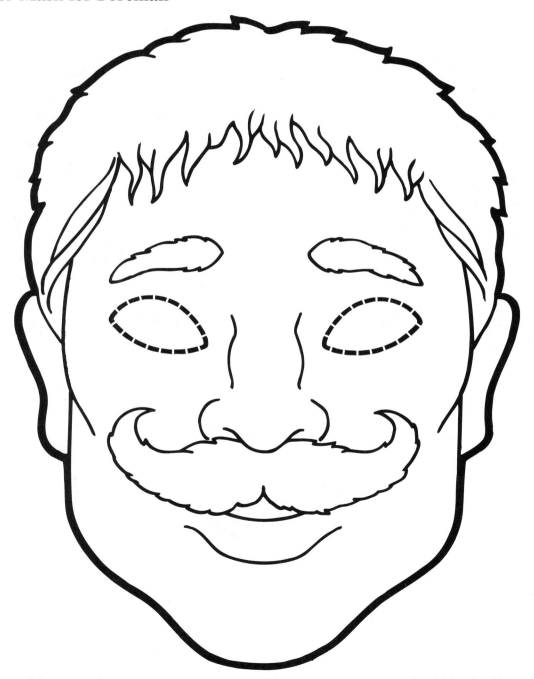

John Henry, Mighty Steel Driving Man (cont.)

Character Mask for Blacksmith

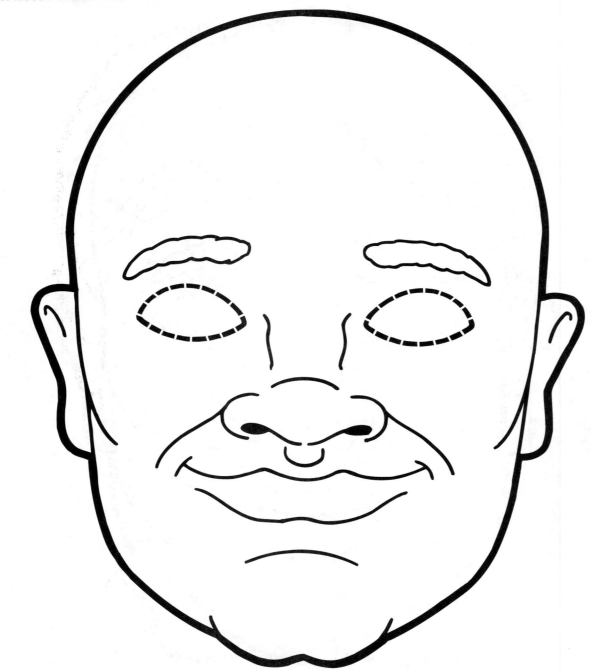

John Henry, Mighty Steel Driving Man *(cont.)*

Character Mask for Salesman

Sally Ann Thunder Ann Whirlwind

An American Tall Tale from the Kentucky Blue Ridge Mountains

Readers' Theater for Six or More

Theme

Girls can, too!

Roles

Narrator 1 & 2, Sally Ann Thunder, Davy Crockett, The Nine Brothers, The Crowd

Tall Tale Summary

Sally Ann was born in the Kentucky Blue Ridge Mountains into of family of nine strapping boys. Sally was the first and only daughter in her family. Those nine brothers were so disappointed at the arrival of the wee baby girl; they began to taunt and tease her. Their shenanigans brought an amazing response from the pretty little girl. Sally Ann promptly hollered so loudly, the house shook right down to its foundation, and the windows shattered into bits. Sally Ann Thunder Ann Whirlwind earned her name by causing a pint-sized thunderstorm and miniature whirlwind from her cradle. As she grew, Sally Ann soundly beat her brothers in all contests of strength and speed because she could out-chat, out-smirk, out-holler, out-paddle, and out-race any child in the Kentucky blue hills. Tales still are told that Sally scared a bear clean out of its hide, she snatched the eagle bald-headed, and she created a tornado of flying alligators.

The tale of Sally Ann Thunder Ann Whirlwind meeting up with Davy Crockett at a barn dance is told most often, however. Sally Ann Thunder Ann Whirlwind had boasted that she would only marry the gentleman who could out-dance her, and she had already danced eight men to the ground, and was still as fresh as a daisy. So Sally and Davy danced and danced and danced all night long and into the next day. Those two did reels and quadrilles and waltzes and whatchamacallits, tangos and fandangos until they had worn out a dozen fiddlers, and they kept on a-dancing until finally Sally Ann Thunder Ann Whirlwind fell down exhausted. She had finally met her match. Davy bent down on one knee, pulled off his coonskin cap, and pleaded with the extraordinary dancing, whirlwind woman to be his wife.

Sally Ann Thunder Ann Whirlwind *(cont.)*

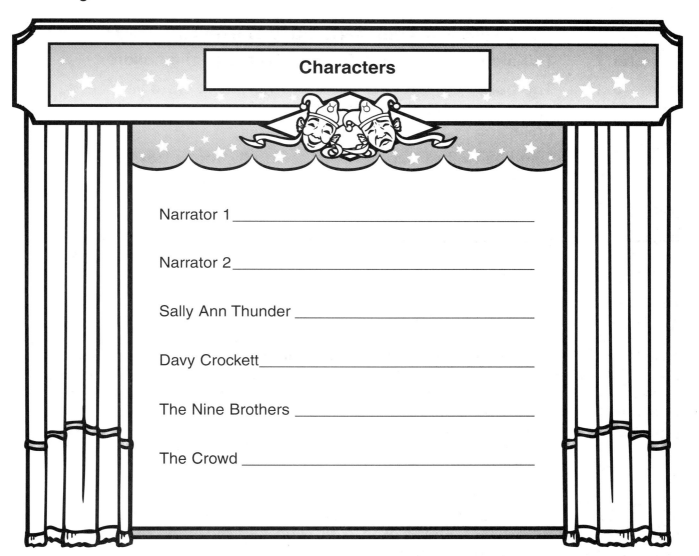

Characters

Narrator 1 _____

Narrator 2 _____

Sally Ann Thunder _____

Davy Crockett _____

The Nine Brothers _____

The Crowd _____

Vocabulary Word List

alligators	gentleman	quadrilles
boast	holler	snatched
curtsey	Kentucky	thunderstorm
disappointed	miniature	tornado
extraordinary	mountains	waltz
fandango	paddle	whatchamacallits
		whirlwind

Sally Ann Thunder Ann Whirlwind

Narrator 1: There once was a wee baby girl born in the Kentucky mountains.

Narrator 2: The moment the child entered this world, she hollered.

Narrator 1: The baby girl had nine older brothers who were very disappointed that this was not brother number 10! And she hollered.

Narrator 2: Can she holler! She hollered so loudly, those boys said the house shook and the window panes shattered.

Narrator 1: They called her Sally Ann Thunder Ann Whirlwind.

Narrator 2: Sally Ann Thunder Ann Whirlwind earned her name causing a pint sized thunderstorm and miniature whirlwind from her cradle.

The Nine Brothers: Can she holler!

Sally Ann: I am Sally Ann Thunder Ann Whirlwind.

The Nine Brothers: Can she holler!

Sally Ann: *(pointing to The Nine Brothers)* My brothers gave me that name because I can out-chat, out-smirk, out-holler, out-paddle, and out-race anyone.

The Nine Brothers: Sally Ann Thunder Ann Whirlwind can out-chat, out-smirk, out-holler, out-paddle, and out-race anyone of us.

Sally Ann: And I can holler!

Narrator 1: The brothers teased Sally Ann Thunder Ann Whirlwind.

Narrator 2: The brothers wanted brother number 10, not a wee baby girl.

The Nine Brothers: Sally Ann Thunder Ann Whirlwind is just a wee baby girl. And can she holler!

Sally Ann Thunder Ann Whirlwind *(cont.)*

Sally Ann: Who are you calling "wee"? I can out-chat, out-smirk, out-holler, out-paddle, and out-race anyone.

Narrator 1: Sally Ann Thunder Ann Whirlwind meant to show her brothers that she could out-chat, out-smirk, out-holler, out-paddle, and out-race any brother in the family.

The Nine Brothers: Sally Ann Thunder Ann Whirlwind scared a bear right out of its fur.

Sally Ann: I can out-chat, out-smirk, out-holler, out-paddle, and out-race anyone.

The Nine Brothers: Sally Ann Thunder Ann Whirlwind snatched the eagle bald-headed.

Sally Ann: I can out-chat, out-smirk, out-holler, out-paddle, and out-race anyone.

The Nine Brothers: Sally Ann Thunder Ann Whirlwind created a tornado of flying alligators.

Sally Ann: I can out-chat, out-smirk, out-holler, out-paddle, and out-race anyone.

Narrator 2: Sally Ann Thunder Ann Whirlwind boasted that she would only marry the gentleman who could out-dance her.

Sally Ann: I can out-chat, out-smirk, out-holler, out-paddle, out-race *and* out-dance anyone.

Narrator 1: Sally Ann Thunder Ann Whirlwind met up with Davy Crockett at a barn dance.

Narrator 2: Sally Ann Thunder Ann Whirlwind had already danced eight men to the ground.

Sally Ann Thunder Ann Whirlwind *(cont.)*

The Nine Brothers: Sally Ann Thunder Ann Whirlwind was fresh as a daisy.

Sally Ann: I can out-chat, out-smirk, out-holler, out-paddle, out-race and out-dance anyone.

Davy Crockett: *(bowing slightly at the waist to Sally Ann)* Miss Sally Ann Thunder Ann Whirlwind, may I have this dance?

Sally Ann: *(with a small curtsey to Davy Crockett)* Yes, indeed, Mr. Davy Crockett. I can out-dance anyone.

Narrator 1:   Sally and Davy danced and danced and danced all night long and into the next day.

Narrator 2:   Sally and Davy danced reels and quadrilles and waltzes and whatchamacallits, tangos and fandangos until they wore out a dozen fiddlers.

The Nine Brothers: They kept on dancing and dancing.

Narrator 1:   Sally and Davy danced and danced and danced all night long and into the next day.

Sally Ann: *(huffing and puffing for breath)* I can out-chat, out-smirk, out-holler, out-paddle, out-race and out-dance anyone.

Davy Crockett: *(huffing and puffing for breath)* Yes ma'am. And I can out-dance anyone.

The Nine Brothers: They kept on dancing and dancing.

Narrator 2:   Sally and Davy danced and danced and danced all night long and into the next day.

Narrator 1:   Sally and Davy danced and danced and danced all night long and into the next day.

Narrator 2:   Finally, Sally Ann Thunder Ann Whirlwind fell down exhausted.

Sally Ann Thunder Ann Whirlwind (cont.)

Davy Crockett: *(huffing and puffing for breath)* Yes ma'am. And I can out-dance anyone.

Sally Ann: *(huffing and puffing for breath)* I cannot out-chat, out-smirk, out-holler, out-paddle, out-race and out-dance anyone.

Narrator 1: Sally Ann Thunder Ann Whirlwind has met her match.

The Nine Brothers: *(gleefully and with amusement)* Folks, Sally Ann Thunder Ann Whirlwind has met her match.

Davy Crockett: *(bent down on one knee)* Ma'am, you are an extraordinary dancing, whirlwind woman. Please say that you will be my wife.

Narrator 2: Sally Ann Thunder Ann Whirlwind said that she would be his wife.

Narrator 1: And that is how Sally Ann Thunder Ann Whirlwind became Mrs. Sally Ann Thunder Ann Whirlwind Crockett.

Sally Ann Thunder Ann Whirlwind *(cont.)*

Character Mask for Sally Ann Thunder Ann Whirlwind

Sally Ann Thunder Ann Whirlwind *(cont.)*

Character Mask for Davy Crockett

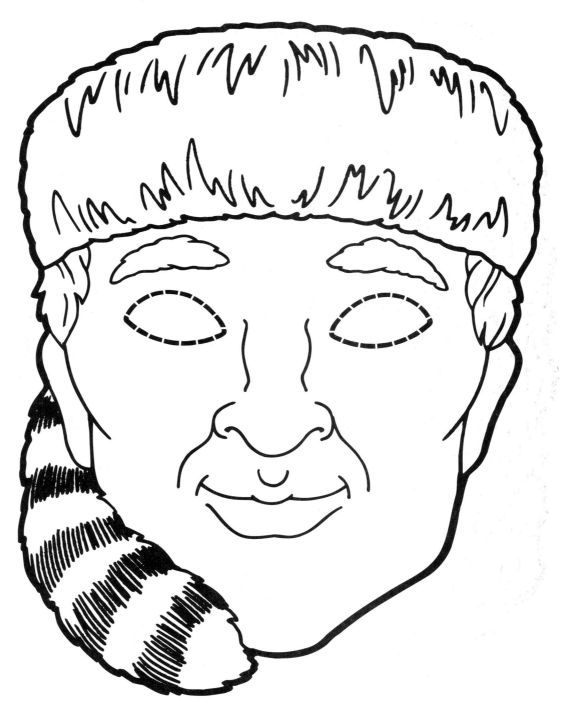

Davy Crockett, King of the Wild Frontier

An American Tall Tale from the Wild Frontier

Readers' Theater for Four Readers

Themes

Patriotism and service to country, fact and fiction

Roles

Narrator 1 & 2, Davy Crockett, President of the United States

Tall Tale Summary

In the early years of our nation, Davy Crockett was well known for all of his wonderful and amazing exploits on the wild frontier. Davy Crockett was born on a mountaintop in Tennessee. He was a rugged frontiersman who befriended the Natives and helped keep the peace between them and the settlers. Folks have heard of Davy wrestling a bear, dancing with Sally Ann Thunder Ann Whirlwind for days without stopping, and fighting bravely at the Alamo. Every single word is true, unless it is false. Crockett was the greatest woodsman who ever lived, who could whip 10 times his weight in wildcats and drink the Mississippi River dry. Few people know of his more amazing service to our nation in Congress. Of course, Davy Crockett was elected because of his extreme bravery. Davy Crockett was called upon to solve all kinds of monumental problems to make this a better nation.

The big freeze of Seventeen-Aught-Something…no maybe, Eighteen-Something-Or-Other was one such monumental problem. It snowed and snowed and snowed for days on end. And it was the end of July. Everything across the country froze solid. It was so cold that whenever anybody would say something, their words just froze in midair. To know what the legislators were a-saying in Congress, they'd have to pluck their words down out of the air, pop the frozen words into the oven, and toast them well done. Now, the President of the United States came to Davy in response to this terrible national crisis and pleaded for his help. Davy knew he could solve this monumental problem. Davy mounted up on his faithful steed, and rode off to the North Pole, where all cold weather comes from. Halley's Comet had passed too close to the Earth that month, and the comet's tail became all tangled up in the North Pole, so the Earth was stuck in place, and couldn't rotate on its axis like it was supposed to. Davy grabbed a hold of the tail end of that comet and untangled it from the North Pole, and then he twirled it around his head like a slingshot. It went a-flying out into space like a stone. And by the time Davy arrived back to Washington, D.C., all the trees were a-blossoming again, and all of the rivers were a-flowing again.

Davy Crockett, King of the Wild Frontier *(cont.)*

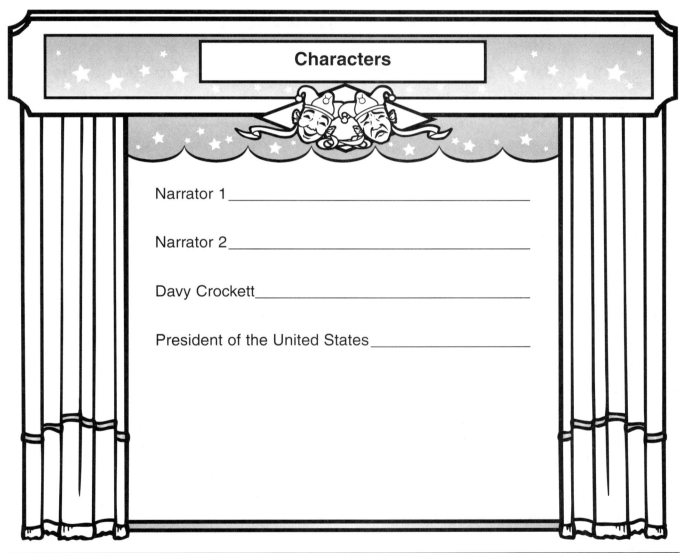

Characters

Narrator 1_____

Narrator 2_____

Davy Crockett_____

President of the United States_____

Vocabulary Word List			
axis	faithful	monumental	steed
bravery	false	represent	Washington, D.C.
Congress	feller	representative	woodsman
cowpuncher	fiction	seventeen	wrestling
eighteen	lumberjack	slingshot	

Davy Crockett, King of the Wild Frontier

Narrator 1: Now you have heard of Paul Bunyan, Pecos Bill, and John Henry.

Narrator 2: All those fellers are fiction. Now Davy Crockett, King of the Wild Frontier, is all fact.

Narrator 1: All fact! Except the parts that are made up.

Narrator 2: All fact! Every word is true.

Narrator 1: All fact! Unless it is false.

Narrator 2: There is the story about Davy drinking the Mississippi River dry.

Narrator 1: Made up!

Narrator 2: There is the tale about Davy wrestling a bear down to the ground.

Narrator 2: Fiction!

Narrator 1: Well, then there is the story about Davy beating 10 times his weight in wildcats.

Narrator 2: False!

Narrator 1: Well, what about the story of Davy in Congress?

Narrator 2: True! Fact! Davy did represent the great state of Tennessee in Congress.

Narrator 1: Of course, Davy Crockett was elected to Congress because of his extreme bravery.

Narrator 2: True! Fact! Davy was extremely brave.

Narrator 1: And he solved the monumental problems facing our nation. There was the time he unstuck the earth frozen on its axis.

Narrator 2: Fiction! False! All made up! But it is a great tale.

Davy Crockett, King of the Wild Frontier *(cont.)*

Narrator 1: Let me introduce Davy Crockett. He can help me tell this story.

Davy Crockett: Howdy, Ladies and Gents! I am Davy Crockett, King of the Wild Frontier.

Narrator 1: Now Paul Bunyan was the greatest lumberjack that ever was.

Narrator 2: Pecos Bill was the greatest cowpuncher that ever was!

Davy Crockett: *(pointing to himself)* But Davy Crockett was the greatest woodsman who ever lived.

Narrator 1: In Congress, Davy Crockett was called upon to solve some of the monumental problems facing our nation.

Davy Crockett: Like the monumental problem back in Seventeen-Aught-Something or maybe it was Eighteen-Something-Or-Other.

Narrator 2: Was that the monumental problem of the big freeze?

Davy Crockett: It snowed and snowed and snowed for days on end. And it was the end of July.

Narrator 1: And that's when the President of the United States came to you?

Davy Crockett: We had a monumental problem. Everything across the country froze solid. The President came to me and said. . .

President: Davy Crockett, we have a monumental problem. Everything across the country is frozen solid.

Davy Crockett: It was so cold that whenever anybody would say something, their words just froze in air.

President: Davy Crockett, the words of the representatives are freezing in air as they try to run Congress.

Davy Crockett: To know what the representatives were saying, they'd have to pick their words out of the air, pop the frozen words into the oven, and cook them to well done.

Davy Crockett, King of the Wild Frontier *(cont.)*

President: Davy Crockett, I am certain that you can solve this monumental problem.

Davy Crockett: Ladies and gents, I knew I could solve this monumental problem.

Narrator 2: What did you do?

Davy Crockett: Ladies and gents, this monumental problem required action. I got on my faithful steed and rode north.

Narrator 1: Why did you ride north?

President: He rode north because that is where all cold weather comes from, of course!

Narrator 2: What happened then?

Davy Crockett: I found the reason for our monumental problem. Halley's Comet had passed too close to the Earth, and the comet's tail was all caught up in the North Pole

President: The Earth was stuck in place, and couldn't spin on its axis like it was supposed to.

Narrator 1: What did you do?

Davy Crockett: I grabbed a hold of the tail end of that comet and undid it from the North Pole.

President: And then he twirled it around his head like a slingshot. It went flying out into space like a stone.

Davy Crockett: By the time I arrived back to Washington, D.C., all the trees were blossoming again, and all of the rivers were flowing again.

Narrator 1: Is this story fiction? Is it a tall tale?

President: All fact! Except the parts that are made up.

Davy Crockett: All fact! Every word is true.

President: All fact! Unless it is false.

Davy Crockett, King of the Wild Frontier *(cont.)*

Character Mask for the President of the United States

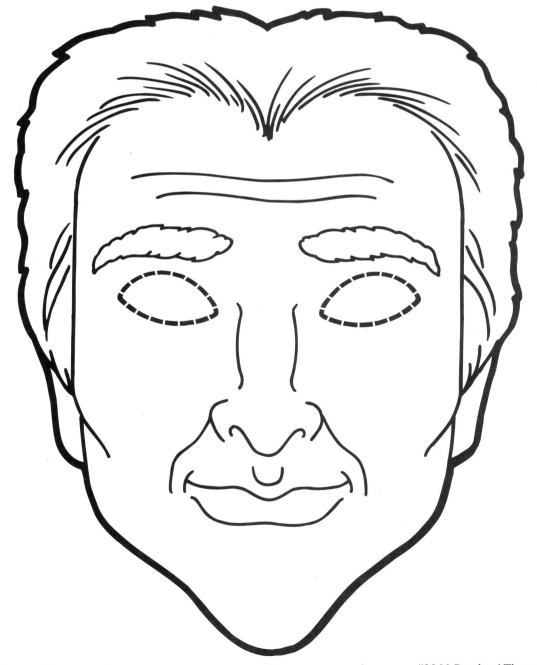

Mike Fink, River Wrestler and King of the Keelboatmen

An American Tall Tale from the Mississippi River

Readers' Theater for Six to Eight Readers

Theme

Succeeding against the odds

Roles

Narrator 1 & 2, Mother Fink, Mike Fink, The Salesman, The Crowd

Tall Tale Summary

During the wild days when America was a young country, it is said that the most daring frontiersmen lived and worked along the rivers. These rugged individuals were the keel boat men who carried cargos of supplies up the Mississippi, the Missouri, and the Ohio rivers. The crewmen of these barges boasted of their grit and superhuman might. Fantastical stories were told of the dangers these keel boat men had overcome, and the extraordinary creatures they had subdued including the story of Mike Fink. Mike could out-pole, out-do, and out-wrestle, out-run, out-jump, out-shoot, out-brag, and out-fight, rough-an'-tumble, no holds barred, anyone or anything on both sides of the river from Pittsburgh to New Orleans.

When Mike was still an infant, his mother decided it would be best to raise this wild man-child on the frontier. On the frontier, Mike could run free without causing an uproar. Mike grew up strong, sturdy, and stout. He won wrestling matches with much older boys and could aim and fire a rifle that was bigger than he was. And he was such a crackerjack shot; he could shoot the flame off a candle. When an enterprising hair tonic salesman spilled his hair tonic in the river, Mike developed a new method of catching fish. He would put out a red and white barber pole on the keel of the river barge and waited with some scissors. He would call out, "Get your free shave and a hair cut here." All the fish whose fur had grown too long or who needed their beards trimmed would hop right out of the water and be picked up.

Mike Fink, River Wrestler and King of the Keelboatmen *(cont.)*

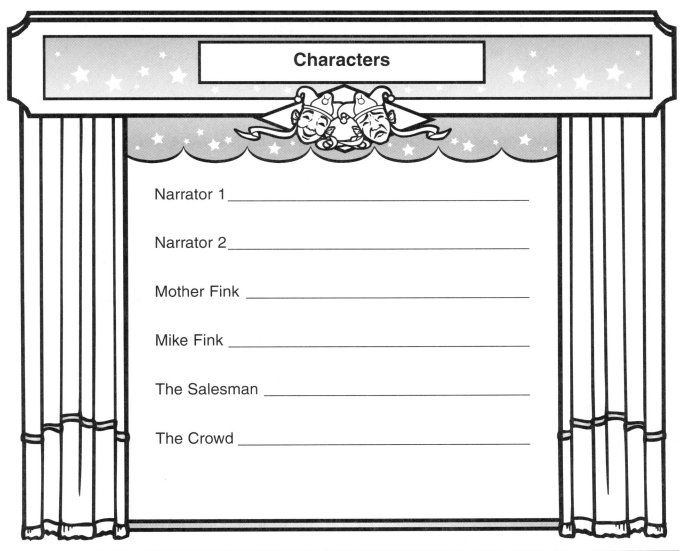

Characters

Narrator 1 _____

Narrator 2 _____

Mother Fink _____

Mike Fink _____

The Salesman _____

The Crowd _____

Vocabulary Word List		
Allegheny	Kentucky	stout
confined	Mississippi	sturdy
crackerjack	mountains	uproar
frontier	restless	wrestle
keelboatmen	salesman	

Mike Fink, River Wrestler and King of the Keelboatmen

Narrator 1:   Mike Fink was born in the Allegheny Mountains.

Narrator 2:   Mike Fink hated being confined as an infant.

Narrator 1:   Mother Fink tried to keep him in his cradle,

Narrator 2:   . . . and to keep him in his clothes.

Mother Fink: *(wringing her hands to the audience)* Dearie me, I tried. But that baby boy ran away from home when he was two days old. Mike Fink is the restless type.

Narrator 1:   His grandpa went searching for him and found him playing leap frog with the toads down by the river.

Mother Fink: *(wringing her hands to the audience)* Dearie me, I tried. But that baby boy fought being indoors so hard that he jumped right through the roof. Mike Fink is the restless type.

Narrator 2:   Mother Fink decided then and there that it would be safest to try to raise her restless baby boy on the frontier.

Mother Fink: *(wringing her hands to the audience)* Dearie me, I tried. But on the frontier, Mike Fink could run free without causing an uproar in the neighborhood. Mike Fink is the restless type.

Narrator 1:   Mike Fink grew up strong, sturdy, and stout on the frontier.

Narrator 2:   Mike Fink wrestled with much older boys but managed to pin them to the ground in seconds.

Mother Fink: *(wringing her hands to the audience)* Dearie me. Mike Fink was such a crackerjack shot, he could shoot the flame off a candle. Mike Fink is the restless type.

Narrator 1:   Mike Fink grew up strong, sturdy, and stout on the frontier.

Narrator 2:   Mike Fink was strong enough to pull a plow and to clear a field while the oxen would take a rest break.

Mike Fink, River Wrestler and King of the Keelboatmen *(cont.)*

Mother Fink: *(wringing her hands to the audience)* Dearie me. Mike Fink is the restless type.

Narrator 1: Mike Fink decided he wanted to be a keelboatman. He wanted to pole cargo barges up and down the Mississippi River with other keelboatmen.

Mike Fink: *(grinning to audience)* That's me! I am Mike Fink! I can out-pole, out-wrestle, out-shoot, out-brag, and out-fight anyone or anything on both sides of the river.

Narrator 2: Mike Fink competed with other keelboatmen for the honor of wearing a red feather. It meant Mike was the strongest of the crew.

Mike Fink: *(grinning to audience)* I can out-pole, out-wrestle, out-shoot, out-brag, and out-fight anyone or anything on both sides of the river. I don't have just one red feather in my hat. I wear lots of red feathers in my hat.

Narrator 1: Mike Fink was the strongest of the crew. Mike Fink was the smartest of the crew.

Mother Fink: *(wringing her hands to the audience)* Dearie me. Mike Fink is the restless type.

Mike Fink: There was the time the hair tonic salesman from Kentucky came out west to make his fortune.

Salesman: Why yes, I do recall that occasion like it was yesterday. I was headed across the river with bottles of hair tonic under my arm.

Mother Fink: *(wringing her hands to the audience)* Dearie me. And you slipped and dropped two bottles of hair tonic into the river.

Salesman: Why yes, I do recall that occasion like it was yesterday. The bottles broke, and the hair tonic spilled into the stream.

Mike Fink, River Wrestler
and King of the Keelboatmen *(cont.)*

Mother Fink: *(wringing her hands to the audience)* Dearie me. Mike Fink developed a new method for catching fish.

Mike Fink: I put out a red and white barber pole on the keel of the river barge and waited with some scissors.

Narrator 2: What happened when you put the barber pole on the keel of the barge and waited?

Mike Fink: I called out, "Get your free shave and a hair cut here. Get your free shave and a hair cut here."

Narrator 1: What happened when you called out "Get your free shave and a hair cut here"?

Salesman: Why yes, I do recall that occasion like it was yesterday. All the fish whose fur had grown too long or who needed their beards trimmed would hop right out of the water.

Narrator 2: Mike Fink would just pick those furry fish up until he caught his limit.

Mike Fink: *(grinning to audience)* I can out-pole, out-wrestle, out-shoot, out-brag, and out-fight anyone or anything on both sides of the river.

Mother Fink: *(wringing her hands to the audience)* Dearie me. Mike Fink is the restless type.

Mike Fink, River Wrestler and King of the Keelboatmen *(cont.)*

Character Mask for Mike Fink

Mike Fink, River Wrestler
and King of the Keelboatmen *(cont.)*

Character Mask for Mother Fink

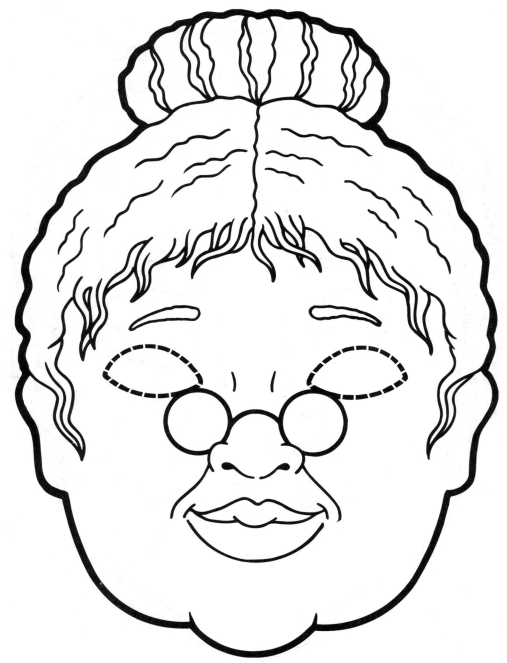

Mike Fink, River Wrestler and King of the Keelboatmen *(cont.)*

Character Mask for the Salesman

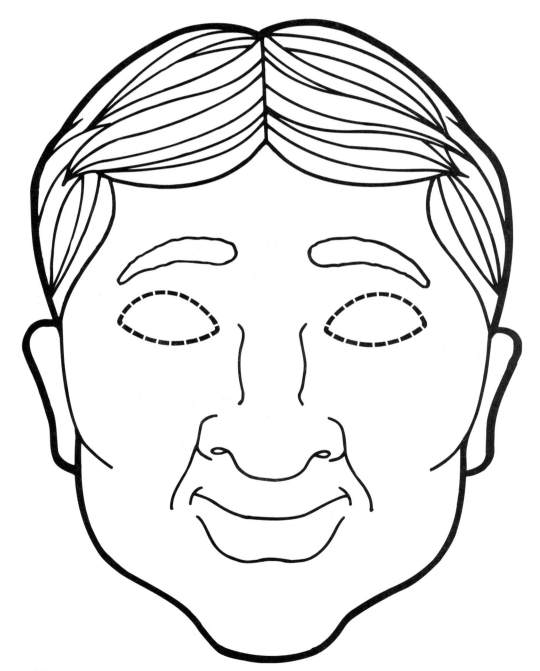

The Legend of Johnny Appleseed

An American Tall Tale from the Ohio River Valley

Readers' Theater for Eight or More

Theme

One person can make a difference.

Roles

Narrator 1, Narrator 2, Johnny Appleseed, Settler 1, Settler 2, Settler 3, Trader, The Crowd

Tall Tale Summary

Johnny Appleseed never wore shoes. He had a tin pot for a hat and a sugar sack for a shirt. He wandered through the wildernesses of Ohio, Indiana, and Illinois with a deerskin sack of apple seeds slung over his shoulder. His name was really John Chapman, but as he traveled and the legends began to spread, everyone began to call him Johnny Appleseed out of love and respect.

Johnny Appleseed began collecting seeds from outside of cider mills. He rode a canoe filled with sacks of seeds down the Ohio river. He walked into the woods to find a place to plant the seeds. Along the way, if he came across settlers, he greeted them happily and gave them some apple seeds. Sometimes he never saw another person, but he didn't mind; he had the birds and the squirrels to keep him company. When he came to a clearing, he would plant some apple seeds and tell the birds not to eat the seeds, but to wait for the apple orchards to grow. And as the story goes, the birds would listen to him!

There are many legends about Johnny Appleseed. Some say that he would sleep in a treetop hammock and chat with the birds. Others say that he played with a family of bears. He was kind to all animals. One morning he followed a trail that led him to a village and found himself at a trading post full of people. He began to talk to them about apples. At first they looked at his tin-pot hat and his sugar-sack shirt and they laughed at him. But as he stood there and talked about apples, they couldn't help listening to him. He gave them apple seeds and they offered to trade them for food. But he just wanted the sick old horse tied up out front. He nursed the horse back to health and took it to a stream to wash it and help it drink.

As he stood there with the horse, Johnny Appleseed heard a whimpering noise coming from the nearby woods. Johnny ran through the trees, following the cries until he came across a giant black wolf with his leg caught in a trap. Johnny freed the wolf's leg and made a splint for it.

Johnny nursed the horse and the wolf back to health, and as he journeyed across the American frontier, the horse and wolf were his constant, loyal companions.

The Legend of Johnny Appleseed *(cont.)*

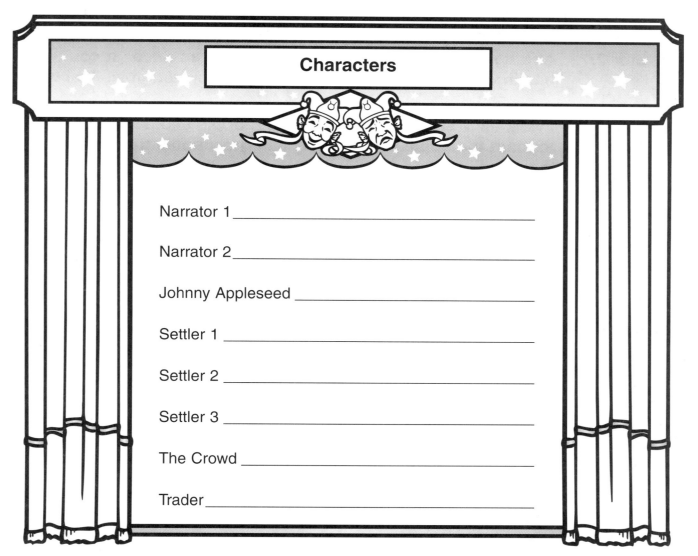

Characters

Narrator 1 _____

Narrator 2 _____

Johnny Appleseed _____

Settler 1 _____

Settler 2 _____

Settler 3 _____

The Crowd _____

Trader _____

Vocabulary Word List

seeds	clearing	hobbled
wilderness	hammock	journeyed
slung	trail	loyal
canoe	trading post	companion
cider mills	whimpering	
orchard	splint	

The Legend of Johnny Appleseed

Narrator 1: Johnny Appleseed never wore shoes. He wore a tin pot for a hat and an old flour sack for a shirt.

Narrator 2: A rattlesnake tried to bite Johnny Appleseed once. It couldn't bite through the skin on his foot. That's how tough his feet were!

Johnny Appleseed: I walk all over the frontier giving out apple seeds. I tell people to plant the apple seeds. They can grow apple trees and feed their families.

Narrator 1: Johnny Appleseed collected seeds from outside cider mills. He filled giant sacks with seeds.

Narrator 2: Johnny Appleseed took the seeds in a canoe. He rowed his canoe down the Ohio river. Sometimes he saw settlers fishing along the banks of the river.

Johnny Appleseed: Seeds! Apple seeds! Here, take some apple seeds! Plant the seeds and grow apple trees.

Settler 1: He once rowed up in a canoe and handed me apple seeds. He told me to find a nice, sunny clearing and plant the seeds. Then I would have apples to feed my family.

Johnny Appleseed: You can plant a whole orchard of apple trees.

Narrator 1: There are many legends about Johnny Appleseed.

Settler 2: I heard that he would sleep in a hammock up in the trees and chat with the birds.

Settler 3: I heard that he once played with a family of bears. He was kind to all animals.

Settler 2: When he planted seeds, he would tell the birds not to eat the seeds. He told them to wait for the apple orchards to grow.

Settler 3: And the birds would listen to him!

Narrator 1: One day Johnny Appleseed followed a trail and found himself in a village. He walked into a trading post full of people.

The Legend of Johnny Appleseed *(cont.)*

Johnny Appleseed: Hello, everyone! I'm here to teach you all about apples.

The Crowd: Look at his hat! It's a cooking pot! Look at his shirt! It's an old sugar sack! What can he possibly teach us about apples?

Narrator 2: As Johnny talked to the crowd, they stopped looking at his hat and his shirt. They started listening to what he was saying. Soon they all crowded forward to take his apple seeds. The Trader, who owned the trading post, offered to trade for the seeds.

Trader: I'll trade you food for your apple seeds. I'll give you coffee and cornmeal.

Johnny Appleseed: I don't need any food today. I would like to trade you my apple seeds for the horse tied outside.

Narrator 1: The horse tied outside was old and didn't look like he could walk another step.

Trader: *(laughing)* That horse? Sure, I'll trade you for that horse.

Narrator 2: Johnny Appleseed took the horse to a stream and washed it and helped it drink. As he stood there in the water, he heard a whimpering noise.

Johnny Appleseed: That sounds like it's coming from the woods.

Narrator 1: Johnny ran through the trees until he found a giant black wolf with his leg in a trap. He bent down to try to free the wolf's leg from the trap. He wasn't afraid that the wolf would bite him.

Johnny Appleseed: I'll get your leg free, my friend.

Narrator 2: Johnny freed the wolf's leg from the trap. He made a splint for the wolf's injured leg. Johnny walked back to the stream. The wolf hobbled behind him.

Narrator 1: Johnny nursed the horse and the wolf back to health. As he journeyed across the American frontier, the horse and the wolf were his loyal companions.

The Legend of Johnny Appleseed *(cont.)*

Character Mask for Johnny Appleseed

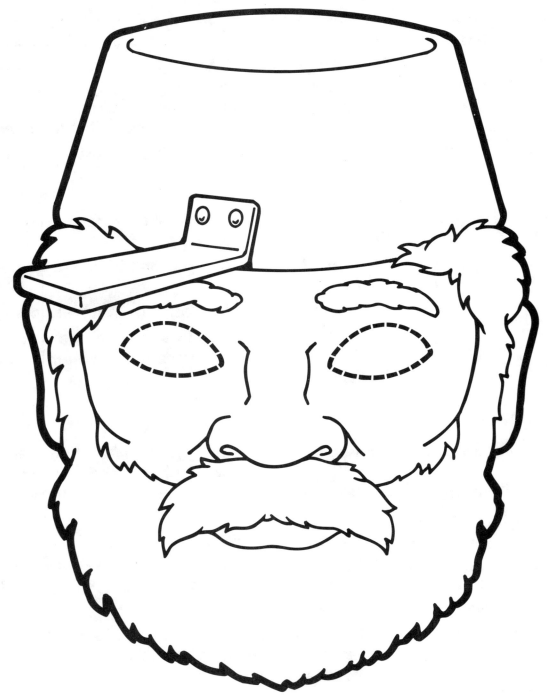